Me, Myself, and Chocolate

A Chocoholic's Guide To Living A Proverbs 14:1 Life

By Kate Bancroft

www.My141Life.com

Book Versions
KDP Paperback ISBN: 979-8-366217-88-0
Ingram Spark Paperback ISBN: 978-1-946265-41-8

Book Layout By Dara Rogers

Copyright © 2022 Kate Bancroft

All rights reserved. No part of this book may be reproduced in any form without prior written permission from the publisher. This work represents the views and opinions of the author alone. No liability in conjunction with the content or the use of ideas connected with this work is assumed by the publisher.

THE HOLY BIBLE, NEW INTERNATIONAL VERSION®, NIV® Copyright © 1973, 1978, 1984, 2011 by Biblica, Inc.® Used by permission. All rights reserved worldwide.

"New International Version" and "NIV" are registered trademarks of Biblica, Inc.®.

Contents

Chocoholic	5
Freedom Calls	15
Mirror Mirror	19
Kissing Sugar Goodbye	29
Smiling on the Outside	37
Little Foxes	43
Mount Rushmore	53
Chasing Perfection	63
Who Are You Looking At?	73
The Fairest	83
Peace Treaty	93

Chocoholic:
a person who is addicted to or excessively fond of chocolate

Driving home from work, the sky was black from the storm. Tears were pouring from my eyes as fast as the rain hitting the windshield. I was a mess, pure misery. Hives, the size of my fingers, had once again taken over.

My doctor had no answer for me. I was sent to a dermatologist who only treats what he can see and of course when I was there, there were no hives! Having no clue as to what is causing them, how can I make an appointment that takes place when I am having issues (hint: that is why I went to the doctor)?

My mom suggested keeping a food journal to determine if there was a connection to this cycle of hives. Both my mom and her sister had problems with chocolate which gave them headaches. Headaches and hives are not the same thing! Desperate for relief, willing to try anything, I began. Quickly, the culprit became obvious. This had to be a mistake! Something so dear to me could never be the problem. I couldn't be expected to live without it.

On the way home, having had an exceptionally rough day, I stopped to get something to take the edge off. After all, I needed it with the day I had. My answer to my problem was, of course, chocolate. Every woman knows that chocolate solves everything! I was not yet finished with my chocolate when my new friend Hives arrived to torture me. The nightmare was true—chocolate was behind this sinister plot of misery. "Just stop eating it" said my husband. What does he know? He cannot possibly understand! He has never had PMS! I'm a "give me your chocolate and no one gets hurt" kind of woman.

I struggled for months knowing it was chocolate that was causing the hives. I said I wouldn't eat it, but couldn't seem to stop. I would lie about eating it, hide it, sneak off to have some. Who was I trying to fool? Hello! Hives everywhere! The only 12 step program for chocolate lovers is to never be more than 12 steps away from it.

The day came when I just couldn't take anymore. Sitting in my car with a candy bar, covered in hives, face drenched with tears, I was feeling hopeless. I had reached the end of myself. I cried out to God, I wanted to stop but I couldn't do it. I wasn't strong enough.

I heard a voice in my head that was so clear and so peaceful say "But I can." It was like a life line to a drowning person. I was so new in my faith in God that I didn't even know I could ask Him for help. When I heard that He could, I did something that I didn't know you really shouldn't do—I said "Okay God, go for it and this is how it needs to be done!" In His mercy, He covered me in grace and I have been a recovering "chocoholic" for over 20 years.

My "love affair" with food began years earlier. I was playing summer league softball. I had missed a ball at home plate and had to run after it. I heard a woman in the stands laugh and say "That's okay, she needs the exercise! She's rather chubby!" When I got home, I weighed myself, choose a number that sounded the opposite of chubby and stopped eating. I was in total control of everything

CHAPTER ONE - *CHOCOHOLIC: A PERSON WHO IS ADDICTED TO OR EXCESSIVELY FOND OF CHOCOLATE*

that went into my mouth until my parents realized something was wrong and demanded that I eat (at the cost of all I held dear had I refused). I perfected the art of eating in front of them then removing everything I had just eaten. This crazy cycle went on for years. Just to make my life more interesting, binge eating joined the party. I was one talented, multi-faceted, mixed-up eating disorder diva.

So, what does this have to do with fear? In my journey to find freedom from eating disorders, I can tell you, for me, it has everything to do with fear: fear of not fitting in, fear of not being good enough, fear of being laughed at, and all pieces of the fear of rejection.

Growing up, I had a speech problem. I was quite difficult to understand and was picked on a lot. In the third grade, we had to tell the class what we would remember most about the person sitting next to us if they were to die tomorrow. I know: great assignment for an 8-year old. The girl I was seated next to told the class that the only thing she would remember about me was the funny way I talk. Everyone laughed. Even the teacher chuckled, before she caught herself. I just wanted to disappear.

That was the final straw for me. I decided that I would stop talking in school, that I would never allow myself to be put in the position to be laughed at, and that I would become invisible. This is how I would survive. Keep my head down and don't make eye contact. The woman at the softball game had no idea what her chuckle and her words did to me.

Can you hear that hurt little girl who made those decisions? She stood up behind the big, thick walls she built and screamed "Not going there again! Not happening! Not on my watch!" She went into full blown protection mode. Did I know why I reacted as

I did? Now I do, but then, all I could do was react out of my fear.

My fear of people laughing at me was the heart of my response. It wasn't my fear of being fat. Before that day being fat had never crossed my mind. So, thanks for that new one! It was that fear of rejection that fueled my eating disorders. Food never rejects you, never hurts your feelings, never makes you feel unworthy and never laughs at you. I can eat when I want, what I want, and how I want. I am in control. If I have control, then I am safe.

In the book of Exodus, God calls Moses to free the Israelites from Egypt. Moses has a long list of reasons why he can't go. "I'm slow of speech. They won't listen to me. Who am I to go?" He is full of 'supposes and what if's." Can you hear it—the fear of rejection, failure, and not being good enough? Going back to Egypt brings up the reasons he had left which he had not resolved. He had been comfortably living in Midian these past 40 years. We mistake comfort for safety from our fear. In truth, it keeps us stuck in our fear.

Moses did return to Egypt. God enlisted Aaron to help Moses move forward. As Moses followed God's direction, with every act of obedience, his confidence became stronger and his fears became smaller. Courage isn't the absence of fear. It is action you take while you are afraid.

As John Wayne said: "Courage is being scared to death but saddling up anyway."

In Exodus 14, the Israelites are freed from slavery. Moses is leading them to the promise land. Panic hits the camp when they realize the Egyptians were after them. Fear spreads and they cry out that it would have been better to serve the Egyptians then to be free. The joy of God delivering them is pushed aside. They are on the way

CHAPTER ONE - *CHOCOHOLIC: A PERSON WHO IS ADDICTED TO OR EXCESSIVELY FOND OF CHOCOLATE*

to the Promise land and fear has them wanting to quit and run for cover. All they can see is the Red Sea before them and the Egyptian army behind them. The situation looks hopeless. Moses goes before the Lord to seek guidance. God responds, "Quit whining!" (Kate paraphrase!) Tell the people to move forward." Forward seems wrong, there is no way there. The only way out is to go back. They do move forward, Moses raises his staff and stretches out his hand as the Lord instructed. The Red Sea parts and they are saved.

Movement forward through our fear brings breakthrough from the fear.

We all have fear. We need to face our fear. Some of us hang out with it, give it a massage, decorate a room for it, and treat it like a pet.

In my high school, speech class was a requirement for graduation. I couldn't figure out why people were so upset. I thought it would be an easy class. After all, I spent 8 years in speech therapy. Imagine my first day in class when I discovered Speech class meant I had to get up in front of the entire class and talk.

My fear was all over me, consuming me as I begged (and begged) my parents to get me out of this class! I remember my dad saying "Katie, if you want to graduate you are just going to have to figure it out." Figure it out! What was there to figure out? Who cares if I graduate! I was not going to do it. There had to be a way out.

Our first assignment was a 3-minute speech. I was sick, scared, couldn't breathe, and sure I was going to die right there in front of the whole class. Keeping my eyes on the floor, I mumbled my way through about 30 seconds before I ran back to my seat crying. I put my head down on my desk and waited for the laughter. Only silence followed. With my head down, I watched the next person.

With each speech, I sat up a little higher. I realized they were just as scared as I was. Not one person was comfortable up there. There were more than a few that looked like they were going to be sick. It was a great day as I realized I was not the only one in the "scared to talk in front of people" club.

The speech class opened a door to a world I didn't know existed. I didn't have to live in fear of talking to people. I had spent so long being ashamed of who I was and not wanting to be me that I didn't know anything about me. I began to gain the confidence to put myself in front of people.

Today, I speak in front large groups all over and enjoy every minute. It is truly part of my DNA. In a group, unless they are booing and throwing things, it's easy to share my journey to freedom.

Philippians 4:13 "I can do all things through Christ who gives me strength."

2 Corinthians 12:9 "My grace is sufficient for you, for My strength is made perfect in weakness."

I am continuously amazed how God takes the source of great pain, shame, and struggle and uses it for His glory. My parents had difficulty understanding me. Now God uses my voice to tell others of His goodness!

So, what are you afraid of? Fear can look like Mt. Rushmore—overwhelming in size with 5 faces ready to tell you about your fears, doubts, and worries to get you to give up. I want you to look at FEAR, really look at it. Ask yourself: Why does this make me afraid?

Asking questions about my fear helps me to gain clarity. This exercise helps me get to the root of my true fear. I would love to give

CHAPTER ONE - *CHOCOHOLIC: A PERSON WHO IS ADDICTED TO OR EXCESSIVELY FOND OF CHOCOLATE*

credit to whom it's due for this exercise, but I am not sure where it came from.

I am going to use my softball story in the example to show you the questions in process:

What about the experience made me afraid?

I am afraid they think I am fat.

Okay, why is their thinking you are fat scary?

What if I don't fit in?

Okay, if you don't fit in, why is that scary?

What if they don't like me?

Okay, why is not being liked scary?

They might laugh at me.

Keep asking and move forward. Watch Mt. Rushmore shrink in size and the voices become quieter as you step over and through your fears.

So, what are you afraid of? How are you letting fear manage your life? For me, it comes back to food. We use food for so much more than what it's designed for. We eat when we are sad, happy, stressed, tired, lonely, and the list goes on.

What, you thought chocolate was my only issue? Let's get real. Having only one would be too easy. I love sweets. If it's made of sugar, it's good! Perhaps you have heard of the condition called a "Sweet Tooth?" I have a mouth full of them! Sugar is the next best thing to chocolate! I know I am not the only one with this condition.

I didn't realize it was a problem until I went on a diet. This diet removed all sugar (gasp!) and flour. Do you know that you can be addicted to sugar and it's unpleasant coming off of that wonderful sugar rush? If you don't believe me, just ask my kids. My evil twin took my place for several days. The diet worked, I lost 20 pounds, and felt better than I think I had ever felt. I went back to my old eating habits. Hello caramel-covered, custard-filled Long John. Happy days are here again! Six months later, I was back on the diet and the evil twin once again took up residence.

I heard someone say if you put "it's just" in front of something, it means you have a problem. "It's just sugar. What's the problem?" My problem was it was never enough. I am not the kind of person who can open a bag of cookies and only eat one. How do people do that?! How do you have Halloween candy left at Easter? I would have to throw my son's leftover candy away because he didn't eat it. Whose child is he?!

So I did what any spiritual person would do, I prayed and promised I would change. After all, I can't eat chocolate. A girl has got to have something!

Psalm 18:23b "And I have kept myself from my iniquity. That which causes me to stumble I have to leave behind."

Food—So much emotion is wrapped up around food.

If you are in the stranglehold of an eating disorder, you must seek professional help. There is freedom on the other side.

We make food such a big deal. I hear it so often, "You can't have chocolate? I could never give that up. You have more willpower than I do." Actually, I am the weakest one I know. I believe God has me share this because I need to hear it! I am also gluten-free, sugar-free

CHAPTER ONE - *CHOCOHOLIC: A PERSON WHO IS ADDICTED TO OR EXCESSIVELY FOND OF CHOCOLATE*

and allergic to several things. Now the question is "What can you eat?" So many people act as if life would be over for them, if they couldn't eat something. Oh, that's right, I did that! Is that you too?

Here are 2 verses that helped me walk out of the grip of sugar:

Psalm 18:37 "I have pursued my enemies and overtaken them. Neither did I turn back again until they were destroyed."

Joshua 1:9 "Be strong and courageous."

Lean on His strength and get people around you who will support you.

Run away from anyone who says to you "it's just one____." Just one is taking you back before the starting line. Don't do it.

Do I miss bread? Yes! I was a huge bread fan. I choose not to eat it so I won't be sick for days. It's a mindset—It's not "I can't." It's an "I choose" not to.

Look at what happened to Eve in the Garden. The enemy turned her focus onto the one thing she was not allowed to eat. She lost sight of everything she could enjoy and BAM! Here I am so many years later and I still don't fit in with the crowd. I no longer talk funny. Now, my food choices are "funny."

On my journey with food, I discovered more freedom to be me. I learned how to walk through one thing at a time and stand in victory.

The struggle with chocolate laid the foundation for the path to discover what I truly fear and to recognize the reasons behind my emotions. My fear of rejection - yep it's still there. My mindset has changed. The 8 year old girl in me no longer calls the shots. The choice is all mine. I can step forward or I could pull an Eve and focus on what is a no-go.

I learned how to watch others enjoy what I no longer choose to eat without feeling like I am missing out. It is only food. I look at this from a temporary view point. After all, this isn't my true home. My life here is short compared to eternity. When I get to heaven, I will be free to eat anything that is there. I am certain it will be better than anything I could eat here.

I am asking Jesus if He would have my mother-in-law's sugar cookies and lemon bars waiting for me.

What, no chocolate?!

Freedom Calls

This journey to food freedom begins with a choice. Just like every other change.

Choice- to choose a different path

   - To go for a different outcome

A choice. Sounds so simple. After all we make thousands of choices every day.

What time we get out of bed. What we wear. What we eat. How we want our coffee. What we are going to listen to. How we get to work. Choices we make without even thinking about them.

Why are choices that will build our path to reaching a desire of our heart so difficult to stay with? Are they just too hard? Do we label them, "someday?" Are we not worth the effort? Have we failed too many times before?

Why can't I do this? What is wrong with me?

Those questions pounded my brain. Crumbling any sense of "I can do this" within me. I have tried and failed to many times. Hopeless, worthless, and ashamed of myself. This was where I found myself again. Living amongst the broken-down walls. Really, it shouldn't be a surprise as to why I am out of control again.

Do I want to be made well? What does it look like? What will it take? It has to be different than just another diet. Been there. Now I am back here!

In Acts 3, Peter and John talk to a cripple man at the entrance to the temple. He has been this way his entire life. He knows of no other way. So, he is asking those passing by for cash. What he doesn't realize is that the opportunity to change his life was just 1 choice away. He asks Peter and John for money. This gets their attention and they stop. They tell this man to look at them. Here is his choice to change his life. He can continue asking others, or he can give his full attention to these guys.

What do we do? If, I focus on these guys, I will miss out on what others might give me. Is it worth the risk?

He chooses wisely and puts his focus on them. He is then offered something other than what he has been asking for. He wants cash but is given healing.

I focused on finding the next greatest diet to follow, but what I needed was healing. There was a better way to live.

Was it easy? NO! Yet so worth it!

I wanted freedom and thought a certain number on the scale would give it to me.

Walking in freedom only is possible after the decision to walk toward freedom is made.

How bad do I want it? What am I willing to pay to get it?

Freedom is not free. Freedom costs you your old life, your old way of doing, living, thinking, eating, habits, ect.

Freedom clears out the old and breathes in fresh.

What if I lived like my body was not the enemy? What if? Is it possible? What will it look like? So many questions circle the first one. One I was not sure how to answer but I knew I wanted (desperately needed!) to go there.

That is where freedom begins, in that moment of clarity. This is where everyone begins their journey. Right here, in this "what if."

You have 2 options, yes and no. That's it, just yes or no. Are you looking for a middle because you have tried countless times before, thought why do I bother, wonder how long I will stick to this one, and hundreds of other self-incriminating thoughts steam rolling through your brain.

It's time to choose yes. Get up because you, my friend, are worth the try.

TRY= walk - fall - hang out here - get up - walk - walk - fall - get up.

This cycle repeats. You just keep getting back up. I have heard many say, "Fall down seven and get up eight!"

I have battled the big, ugly food giants for most of my life. The only way to defeat them is in the getting back up. I have had great success and spent far too much time lying face down in the pit. I learned the hard way that on my own I am not strong enough. I had to learn how to put on the whole armor of God to be able to stand and fight. Ephesians 6:10-18, Philippians 3:12-14, Hebrews 12: 1-2.

I want to share with you my tried and true path of Food. Faith. Freedom. This is what keeps me grounded and helps my clients walk in freedom.

It's so simple. (not saying it is easy!) I am amazed at the simplicity of this. I was making it so difficult. Always chasing perfection. It's time to experience freedom!

Mirror Mirror

Cue the evil queen entering her chambers. She approaches the mirror and asks, "Mirror, Mirror on the wall, who is the fairest of them all?"

The mirror replies, "You, my queen, are the fairest of them all."

The queen gives a knowing smile and leaves the room, once again given the assurance of her superiority.

This meeting happens for many years. She is seeking confirmation that she is *People Magazine's* "Most Beautiful Woman." Her life is in order, she is in control, or so she thinks.

Then the day came when the Mirror's reply was different. Someone else had "taken" the title from her. This confirmation statement from the mirror was what she had built her confidence on. This declaration of her "not measuring up" brought out what was truly in her heart.

The bible teaches us, "Out of the overflow of the heart, the mouth speaks."

Her desire to regain what she believed she had lost to another would drive her to destroy the one who took it.

"Comparison is the thief of joy" - Franklin Roosevelt.

This comparison game is as old as humanity. Going back to Genesis, let's look at Cain and Abel. They both brought gifts to the Lord. Abel's gift was accepted and Cain's was not. Cain, out of the overflow of his heart, killed Abel. He didn't like coming in second. He didn't like losing this comparison game.

God shows us what He thinks of this game we play. He put in His "Top 10" Thou shall not covet. Stop focusing on what someone else has that you think is better than what you have.

I know, from my life, a lot about comparing ourselves to others and what it does to us negatively. I spent so much of my life trapped in this game.

How it can send me down the mountain of "I am so not good enough" leaving me wallowing in the pit of "I have nothing to offer." This is where I spent most of my time. In the rehashing of "I am not enough, a mistake, unloved, unwanted, and totally not necessary."

Negative outlooks:

- So not pretty enough
- Lacking any talent
- Sisters are far smarter than I am
- My career is a disappointment
- Not a good enough wife
- I never achieve anything
- Why can't I look like her

CHAPTER THREE - *MIRROR MIRROR*

- I cannot lose weight
- People will laugh at me
- I talk funny
- And the list goes on and on….

Comparing like this is meaningless. We often are not comparing apples to apples. Even if we are really comparing apples to apples, not one of my 3 apple trees produce the same variety of apple nor ripen at the same time. We are looking at our beginning and comparing it to someone's third quarter. It's a losing battle because we are not at the same place in life nor have the same life! Living like this results in anger and disappointment, towards ourselves and towards the one whom we think is beating us. Remember the quote from earlier? Comparison is the THIEF of joy. This comparison robs you of happiness.

I believe that is why the enemy has promoted this type of comparison in our culture. Come with me for a moment…how many "selfies" are taken before one is posted? What was wrong with the 40 other ones? How many "filters" are used to get the best-looking picture? Not perfect? No problem, just take another one. We are obsessed with only posting the best but we compare our real life with others best. Is it any wonder why scrolling through social media rarely brings contentment or gratitude to our lives? Remember, it took them dozens of tries before they posted one. Yet, that's the one we think is real.

What about reality shows? We get sucked in to the "real life" shows. We have to watch who the latest bachelor picks, who has the greatest talent or who will be the survivor. How many celebrity gossips shows and magazines are there? When I asked Google about celebrity gossip magazines 40 came up. Really 40?! All of these draw us into, if we let them, our lives just don't measure up. We are unsuccessful, uninteresting, and unnoticed. They are winning the "Mirror Mirror" question and without us realizing it, we are disappointed with us and know if we could be like them, we would be happy.

Are you ready for good news? Yes, there is good news! While there are many negative thoughts that come from this game, if we pay attention, we find there are positive ones also. We can use comparison as a motivation to improve an area in our life.

- Spiritual growth. Find a truth teaching church, join a bible study or find a mentor to help you. Every one of us needs to be pressing in closer to God. There is not one who "has arrived" or "knows it all." We are all a work in progress.

- See someone with a trait that you want in your life? Ask them how they developed it and try it!

- Know someone who is patient in ways you are not? Ask them how they do it. Seek ways to implement in your life.

- Know someone who is physically fit. Ask them for tips. Get moving and start drinking water.

- Find someone who is growing in an area that you want to improve. Join them! You can do it too.

- Ask your boss or someone you admire, what books they are reading and read one of them.

- Love how one of your co-worker's dress? Ask them for

pointers. Discover your own style.

- Remind yourself that other people's "outsides" cannot be compared with your "insides."

It took years for me to break out of the negative thought cycle of comparing. I was too eager to demean me. I "knew" I was not good enough. I said too many times, "I could never be that because…" and I had an arm length of reasons to back it up.

Here is the foundation I had to learn to stand on to push back at the enemy at his game. I am me. Yep, that's the foundation. Just 3 little words but a lifetime of value. Each and everyone of us are unique. I needed to get a hold of that and not let go of it. I needed to stop trying to be someone else.

Just as the serpent said to Eve, "Did God really say?," he comes at me asking "Did God really make you like that? Wow, did He get it wrong. You will never be…you are not…"

I needed to discover who I am in God's eyes. That I am unique and that because He made me…I am enough because HE IS ENOUGH and I am created in HIS image. So are you. This truth is the same for all of us. In God's vast array of creation, one cannot adequately compare a rose to a redwood tree. Each has their unique purpose and each would fail miserably trying to be like the other. Yet, in this game, we compare each other the same way and think we are lacking.

Newsflash…the one whom you think has it all and you feel less than because of what you think they have/are, feels the same way. Think about that for a moment. All of us struggle in this. ALL. OF. US. Yet, God created all of us in His image. The very one who put the universe together, created the sunrise, filled the meadow with wildflowers, and colored the tropical fish, made you. Yes You! You are beautiful, you are fearfully and wonderfully made. In His eyes, you are the fairest of them all.

In the chapter, "The struggle is real," we talked about putting on the helmet of salvation. Here in the comparison game, it is necessary for your victory. This is where we can begin to recognize the thoughts that are coming in, take note of what they say and evaluate whether they are truth or lies.

Truth is from God.

Building you up. Directing your path. Lines up with scripture. Used for correction.

Lies are from the enemy.

Condemnation. Contrary to scripture. Tears down.

The lies, we just need to release them. Tell them, "NO!" and cover with them with the truth of God's word.

We know how the evil queen reacted to the news from the mirror. She responded from a place of brokenness, pride, power, and anger. We too have a choice how to respond in this game in our life. It's time to get out of the game. Announce your retirement from playing the game.

One of my mom's "momism's" was, "If wishes were horses, then beggars would ride. I must have heard her say it a thousand times and as a kid, I never understood it. I tried begging for what I wanted but being "kid 4" out of 5, they already were well versed in my attempts and it got me nowhere. The point she was trying to make is this, you cannot wish something into existence. Nothing in life is just handed to you. If you want something different than what you have, you will have to work for it. I have heard it said that "doing things the same way but expecting different results is the definition of insanity." Restructuring your position in the comparison game will require you to work at it. You will move out of your "comfort zone" into the "I am changing zone." Change happens incrementally. Change happens one decision at a time. But it happens if you stay the course, lean into God and push through the lies of the enemy.

So how do I make a change?

Where do I start?

We often say "The grass is always greener on the other side" when we are looking at something we think is better than what is on our side of the fence. Let's look at Commandment 10 again. Thou shall not covet.

We look at their grass and marvel at the manicured edges, the deep green color, the lack of dandelions, and the overall perfection of their yard.

Okay, take a step back and stay off their grass! You have no idea what they have done to get their grass to this point. Truthfully, do you really think by having their grass that all your problems will be solved?

Water your own grass!

If you want a healthier looking, dandelion free lawn (life) you need to put in the work. You must change how you care for it.

What are you reading?

I have heard many brag how they have not read a book since they have got out of school. Readers are leaders. Changes require the knowledge of how to change. In order to lead yourself, you must be reading sound teaching material. Ask any successful person how many books they read a year. The excuse "I don't read well or I don't like to read" is no longer viable, audio books are amazing.

What are you spending time on?

Do you spend hours every evening in front of the TV? On the computer or playing games on your phone? Take inventory of your time spent and ask if this improves your life and gets you closer to your goal. If the answer is no, rethink this activity.

Who are you listening to?

I am repeating myself here…is this a voice that lifts up or tears down? Is the information helpful in "watering your grass?"

Stop your "Could've, Should've, Would've's."

Seriously just stop! All of rehashings of I should've done this or I could've been that or the I would've been this are getting us nowhere! Hindsight is 20/20 and by continually looking at the past keeps us from looking ahead. Leave it in the review mirror. Our past is to be learned from not a merry go round to stay on.

Get a big pitcher of grace and pour it on your past.

Your past is probably full of pitfalls, bumps, pain, and regrets. The life experience you have is invaluable for the life you want to live. Pour grace on your past. It's over. You cannot change it. I love the line Rafiki says to Simba in the Lion King. Rafiki hits Simba with a stick and Simba asks him why did he do that and Rafiki says, "it's in the past, what does it matter." What is in our past can still be painful but it is out of our ability to change what happened. We can only move ahead day by day, in the strength that was built, the

CHAPTER THREE - *MIRROR MIRROR*

wisdom gained, and the clarity of vision our past gave us.

Grace- God's riches at Christ's expense.

Leave your past at the feet of the One who died for you. He is the only one who can redeem what needs to be redeemed. His grace covers all. Let Jesus pour it over your life.

You are right here.

Yep, we all start at the same place. The beginning. No one gets to go back to start earlier. Accept where you are today. You are called to run your race, as each one of us are. Your race begins right where you are. Remember, you are here, right now, because the Creator of the Universe wants a relationship with you. Come before Him as you are. Do not wait until you have it all together, that day will never come.

Today, right where you are, come. He is waiting.

You are still here.

If you are reading this then you are still breathing so that means there is still time for you to be used by God. No one knows the time span of their life except God. Give Him every bit of your life. It's not too late, you are not too old, or too messed up. Life is still happening and you have not missed it!

I want to leave you with this, you are more than what a mirror says you are. The number of followers you have on social media nor the number on a scale does not determine your worth. God alone determines your worth.

For God so loved the world, that He GAVE. For you and for me, He gave His one and only son, Jesus so that we could spend eternity with Him.

The evil queen's whole identity was wrapped up in what the mirror said about her. Without her beauty, she was nothing.

Whose standard of beauty are we trying to meat?

In Song of Songs, the bride says "I am dark but lovely."

Yes, I am dark. I, on my own, am left with a prideful, sinful nature.

I am lovely because of the One who loves me enough to save me from me and call me His own.

Kissing Sugar Goodbye

This thought brings many running in terror at the very idea of leaving sugar out of our lives. How is one supposed to live without sugar? I love sweets. I would rather eat dessert as my appetizer all day long.

Maybe you are one of those people who I never understood. The kind who can open a bag of candy, take a few pieces and leave it. I mean, you just walk away. How do you do that?! If I hadn't seen it, I would not have believed it was possible. I would be tormented, hearing it call my name, reminding me that it was still here, waiting for me to come. It would be a focal point in my thoughts, waiting until I could get back to it. I am sure I would have been circling it like a ravenous pack of wolves. Just being a little dramatic. Truth is, I would never leave it until every bite was gone. Didn't matter if was even mine. My kids Halloween and Easter candy disappeared like magic! I could always finish it then go get another one to replace it. Yep, that's the life I was living. A total sugar addict.

Addiction (noun) - The fact or condition of being addicted to a particular substance, thing or activity.

The experts tell us that there are substance addictions and

behavior addictions.

Substance addictions are chemically trigger. Like cocaine, cigarettes, pain killers, caffeine, ect...

Behavioral addictions are usually brought on by an emotional trigger. Like gambling, shopping, eating, ect...

Sugar addiction, however, falls into both categories. It triggers a chemical response (pleasure center in our brain) and a behavioral (emotional need) one. It's a double whammy.

At a church we attended before moving here, we had a locally famous news anchor speak. He talked about his drug addictions, the problems it caused and how with God's help he overcame. I was so impressed. I was cheering loudly on the inside for his bravery. I was also saying, on the inside, that could never happen to me. Here's the new flash, at this time of my life, I am living inside the sugar bowl. I am so good at hiding it that I believe no one knows. Living large in denial! He proceeds to talk about other types of addictions. Then he looked right at me, I am serious, he really did, and said "Don't sit there and think it's only food, it's no big deal. If you are lying about it, hiding it, embarrassed by it, and cannot stop thinking about when you can have it next, you have a problem." I was stunned, angry, and speechless. How did he know what I was going through? I was scared to look around because I was sure everyone could see he was talking to me.

I would LOVE to tell you, that at that moment, my life changed. That God showed up and I was miraculously changed on the spot, right there in front of the entire church. Arms raised and dancing the freedom dance. Changed. Nope. That is not how it happened. I will tell you God did show up in that moment. That seed of truth planted itself deep in my heart and I would never be the same.

CHAPTER FOUR - KISSING SUGAR GOODBYE

Healing isn't always instantaneous or noticeable. Sometimes healing takes time.

Change can only happen when you are willing to be changed. You know, that transformation into Jesus' image. That can only come when you admit you need to change. I was on my soapbox, declaring I have already given up chocolate, wasn't that enough? How can I be expected to sacrifice more?! It did take a few months of the Holy Spirit working on me for me to truly wake up to the reality that sugar was my first love. I had a problem. I came to this realization after polishing off a box of cookies. Sick to my stomach, the slippery slope thought of "just throw up" entered my mind. I thought I had overcome the bulimia. This scared me into action.

In the years since, the veil has been pulled back regarding sugar. Experts will tell you that it is one of the most addictive substances known. The food companies sure know this and use it against us to sell more product. Walk down the cereal aisle at the grocery store. How many sugary cereals, breakfast items, and granola bars are promoted as healthy for us and for our kids? How many grams of sugar are in a single soft drink? In the French fries that we love. It is in almost everything.

Read the labels and you will rarely find the word "sugar." Instead listed are one or more of the dozen other names it has. Sucrose, Dextrose, Corn Syrup, Brown Rice Syrup, Brown Sugar, Organic Cane Juice, High Fructose Corn Syrup, Fructose, Glucose, Coconut Sugar, Palm Sugar just to name a few.

Sugar, that sweet white stuff that comes in a 4# bag in the baking aisle comes from 2 different sources. Either sugar beets, which are mostly gmo's or sugar cane. Both are plants, both grow in the earth.

We know that the enemy likes to imitate God. God created the earth and all that is within it. Satan can only imitate because he cannot create any other that division, disorder. It makes me wonder about these artificial sweeteners out there. Created in a lab with chemicals. Promoted as a great alternative to sugar. He comes disguised as an angel of light. As a new wonderful sweetener that can help us. Studies have shown they are anything but good for us.

Getting off sugar was a bumpy road for me. I quit. Yep, cold turkey. I was following a faith-based program and I signed an agreement that I would be 100% compliant and posted it on the refrigerator for the whole family to see. My body went through withdrawals. Body aches, mood swings, tiredness, crabbiness, hunger, and basically, I was just miserable for days. I couldn't be in the kitchen without rifling through the cabinets looking for something. I did plan ahead and there was nothing there for me to find.

I did it. I followed the plan and it worked. I came through it off sugar, lost 15 pounds, and gained a better understanding of why I eat the way I do. I felt on top of the world.

The enemy is sneaky. He sits in the shadows waiting for the right moment to strike. He knows what worked before and he will come for you. I was totally unprepared for his "gorilla warfare" tactics. I guess I truly believed that the battle was done, finished, over and I won. It started small. Just one bite, no big deal. It didn't take long before I was eating what I shouldn't, thinking I had it all under control.

Control is an illusion. I think the enemy uses that illusion of control to take you deeper into the trap.

I hit bottom faster this time. Recognizing the warning signs as I traveled this road before. I was so discouraged with myself for letting it get me again.

I went through the program again, only this time signed up for longer. Once again, I came through clean of sugar.

Just last week, as I was in the grocery store with my daughter, I said, out of the blue, "caramel corn sounds delicious." She laughed and said "You do not eat caramel corn!" We then had a conversation about homemade caramel corn and how good it is.

Should have seen the warning lights or heard the sirens going off! But, so comfortable in my "I have been doing this for years and I have got this under control," I was no longer looking for warning signs. I had me "under control." A few days later, at a Gluten Free festival, we stopped at a booth that had homemade popcorn in several flavors. Of course, there was caramel corn. I had been thinking about it for days. Where was my helmet? I was letting my thoughts take me captive and had surrendered willingly. I picked up a bag to look at the ingredients. Sugar was the fifth listed. Now in my life, if sugar is fifth or less, I do not worry too much about it because it is nominal amount. This is caramel corn. It's sweet. Maybe the sugar content is low but it's going to be sweet. Did I run away? Nope. I tried a few flavors. I bought a bag, justifying the sugar. You know the justifying trick, right? "Just as if I had not messed up." Well, I messed up! Didn't even realize it until I had pulled my head out of the bag with it stuck in my teeth and all over my fingers. Scratching my head (with sticky fingers) thinking, "How did I get here?" So, today is a new day. I am back to the beginning. It is sugar detox time.

In Proverbs 27:23 says "Be diligent to know the state of your flocks and put your heart into caring for your herd."

Hang with me here. I am not saying I am a sheep. What I am saying is I must be diligent in knowing the situation, the surroundings I am in. Am I vulnerable to the enemy's attempts against me? Am I paying attention, looking for warning signs? This is why we must wear our helmet of salvation. We must take a hard look at our thoughts. Analyze are they for us? Great!!! Against us? Then cover them with the truth and declare the lie has no power over us! Here's the thing, I didn't do that. I allowed the caramel corn thought to hang out in my mind. I let it get bigger, thinking about how good it would taste. The truth is, I should have declared it gone from my mind and that it has no place in my life. Yet, I didn't. I picked up a bag and looked at it! Do you think that helped me? No, it just made the desire stronger. I was not paying attention. I think that's why God has me teaching this to women and sharing my battles. I am the weakest one I know. Here's the most beautiful truth. John asked 3 times to have the thorn in his side removed. He was told that Jesus' grace was sufficient. I love that when I show up in my weakness, Jesus is proved strong. I am weak. I fall down. I am not a failure. Neither are you. I must put my heart into caring for me. By caring for me, I am caring for the rest of my family.

I see sugar like a Goliath in my life. Big, powerful, and looks undefeatable. One big, ugly giant that loves to call out to me to tell me how little I am. How he will defeat me and take my life. Mocking my efforts to stand up and face him.

Cue David in 1 Samuel 17. He is amazed by the lack of response from the army. His own brothers are there and mock him in his desire to do battle. The king doesn't believe in him. I think he gives him his armor just to give David a fighting chance. David knows he cannot fight Goliath in Saul's armor. He has to fight with the weapons he has training on. David picks up his sling and grabs 5

CHAPTER FOUR - *KISSING SUGAR GOODBYE*

stones from a stream. I wish I could see everyone's faces. This is the guy who is going to fight Goliath? We are doomed! No way he will win. He is too small, too young, has no experience, and is absolutely not dressed as a warrior in a battle!

Sounds like the same talk the enemy uses when he talks to me about me. I cannot win because I am not strong enough, talented enough, do not know enough, and when I fail, everyone will see it. Saul, David's brother, and the entire army didn't see David's true weapon. His heart for God. His belief that the Lord God was his shield and armor. He knew God would show up in the battle and give David the victory for God's glory.

Saul was fighting for his glory not God's.

I am able to win against sugar's hold on me because I know who I truly belong to and it is not sugar. To quote David, "I come at you in the name of the Lord God" 1 Samuel 17.

Psalm 18:1-3, 17, 28-29, 32, 37-39, 49.

I love you. Lord you are my strength. The Lord is my rock, my fortress and my savior, my God is my rock, in whom I find protection. He is my shield, the power that saves me and my place of safety. I called upon the Lord, who is worthy of praise and he saved me from my enemies. He rescued me from powerful enemies from those who were too strong for me. You light a lamp for me. The Lord, my God lights up my darkness. In your strength I can crush an army; with my God I can scale a wall. God arms me with strength and he makes my way perfect. I chased my enemies and caught them; I did not stop until they were conquered. I struck them down so they could not get up; they fell beneath my feet. You have armed me with strength for the battle; you have subdued my enemies under my feet. For this, O Lord, I will praise you among the nations. I will sing praises to your name.

Joshua 1:9 "Be strong and courageous! Do not be afraid or discouraged. For the Lord your God is with you wherever you go."

Maybe you are intimidated by the thought of walking away from something that has a hold on you. Maybe it's sugar. Maybe it's shopping, gambling, drinking, gossiping, television, screen time, or one of a thousand others. Thinking how can I possibly navigate life without it. I like it. I enjoy all the wonderful things it brings except for… Only you can fill in this blank. What is this thing costing you? Time with your family? A job? Financial breathing room? What would that be worth to you to be free?

We only change when the pain of staying the same is greater than the pain of change. All change is hard at first. Every step you take in it leads you closer to freedom.

Lev 11: 45 "I am the Lord who brought you up out of the land of Egypt to be your God, you shall therefore be holy for I am holy."

It's time to kiss the sugar (or whatever has a grip on you) goodbye. Leave the land of slavery, put on your armor, and take a step towards freedom.

Smiling on the Outside

I have a friend who, when asked, "How are you?" her reply is "Great, I am doing great." Which, I know, is really is code for, "I am so close to falling apart so don't ask because I will cry and you know how much I hate to cry!"

I cannot tell you how many times I have been a mess but the moment I walk in, my face changes and a smile now where quivering lips were just 5 minutes prior.

Is this how we are to handle our struggles? With fake smiles and hiding?

Maybe we should follow Hollywood's version. We have seen the chick flicks where she gets dumped. Heart-broken, she hides in her apartment for weeks. When her girlfriends finally come to do an intervention, we see her apartment littered with take-out and ice cream cartons.

Maybe, for you, the grocery store is like running the gauntlet. Every isle seems to have a land mine. Your favorite go-to confections leap into your cart, they call your name and do a dance to get your attention. We desperately try to ignore them but their siren call is too much to resist. So, we give in, I mean, why bother to fight it.

I felt like my home front was a battle field. My eating was out of control. I was so skilled in the art of hiding it that I think I was even fooling myself. I was on the emotional gerbil wheel, just going around and around, wanting it to stop but knew I couldn't do it myself.

Shame. So much shame. What is wrong with me? I have a wonderful husband who loves me (but I didn't see how he could because I didn't even remotely like myself) and two beautiful kids. Life should be perfect.

Should be. Two very dangerous words that told me that I am the problem, I do not deserve perfect and I will never be enough.

If anyone should find out how I really am…wow, my life would be over.

So, I hid. Hiding affected every one of my relationships. How do you develop a close lasting relationship when you are desperately working to keep this big bad ugly secret a secret? You don't. You live behind a plastic face, a plastic smile, drowning in tears on the inside, and a secret that is always there, lurking, trying to break free from the shadows.

Oh, how food giants declared "open season" on my mind. Worthless, unlovable, unwanted, weak, hopeless, fraud, shame, and the list, on perpetual repeat.

Maybe, for you, it's not food but something else. Smoking, shopping, gambling, drinking, or countless other things we are allowing control over our lives.

I want you to know, you are not alone in the fight.

This battle ground you are on is not your permanent place. Battle

CHAPTER FIVE - SMILING ON THE OUTSIDE

grounds are meant to be temporary. The enemy comes at us with his bag of tricks (lie, kill, steal, and destroy). He knows where he has had victory over us before so he comes back for more, again, again, and again. He laughs watching us trying to get back up until we just stop trying. He has stolen our hope, our confidence, our identity, and for some, our very lives.

It is time to stand up and wash yourself off. Remove the dust from the battle. Wash yourself with the word of God and rest in His shelter. But know this, the enemy will swing back for another round. His mistake! This time you will be taking him down!

Let's take a close look at what happened. What signs did you see leading up to this Goliath dragging you down?

- Review your emotions.
- Review where you were.
- Review what time of day.
- Review what happened earlier in the day.
- Review what you reached for.
- Review what you said about yourself.

Awareness of how the enemy comes is the first step in blocking him. Remember, he is looking for one he can devour…stop being one!

Do you see the warning signs?

Close your eyes for a moment. Take one of those warning signs and visualize a police car. We all know that we instinctively take our foot off the gas pedal, no matter how fast we are going, when we see one. Now, take the next warning sign and add an alarm to it. Next one, flashing lights. Are you getting the picture? We must pay attention to these warning signs to not be tripped up again.

The good news is, now you are aware of how the enemy is fighting you and how to not be blindsided by his tactics. The bad news is, he will still try to get you to fall because that's what he does. The good news is, if you do fall, you get right back up because you know how it happened.

In Ephesians 6, we are told that we do not wage war against flesh and blood. Our enemy is not flesh and blood. We are given armor to wear in the battle. The battle is real and it begins in the mind. The first piece of armor I want to talk to you about is the helmet of salvation. This is vital! Remember way back to the beginning, in Genesis, how Satan used words to deceive Eve? He is using the same tricks against us. He wants us to think things about ourselves that are contrary to the truth in God's word.

That we are hopeless…nope! Jesus is our hope.

That we are worthless…nope! We are a pearl of great price.

That we can't do this…that's true by ourselves but we have one who gives us strength…Jesus!

That we will never change…nope! We are being transformed into the image of Jesus.

That we will fail…that's true, but our God NEVER fails and his word tells us that he will never leave us or forsake us.

That we are not loved…nope! For God so loved the world that he gave Jesus so we could be called sons and daughters of God.

I spent so many years trying to fight this on my own. It was exhausting! I finally, (I know what took me so long?!) one day asked myself, "What would my life look like if I stopped treating myself as if I were the enemy?"

I am not my enemy. You are not your enemy.

The enemy is the enemy. He can be beat!

I changed how I view the struggle. I began to focus on what God told the Hebrews to do when they were caught between the red sea and the Egyptian army. They were scared, knowing in this place, they were easy pickins for the Pharaoh. Defenseless against the army. They had no weapons, no training, and now up against the best army in the world. It reminded me of me and how I felt caught in this battle, defenseless and weaponless. Staying here, I would continue to be easy pickins for the enemy. When Moses went to God for direction, God said, "Tell the people to move forward." Ummmm, there's a great big sea ahead of them? God's direction does not always make sense to us. I wonder if the Hebrews thought, "Does Moses see this ahead of us? What are we to do?"

Here's the thought, The Hebrews could have stayed and faced the army and lost and gone back into bondage…not where anyone truly wants to be. God told them to move forward. God was freeing them from slavery. Their freedom was in moving forward. So, am I staying, waiting to be beat or am I going to move ahead and chase this freedom God promises?

Yep, I am choosing to chase freedom!

I changed how I do battle.

The awareness of how the enemy does battle, the truth of who I am in God's eyes, hiding His holy word in my heart and wielding the weapons he designed for me bring me to a place of victory. Not because I am anything special or have marvelous will power. It's because of one thing…I began to chase freedom. In chasing freedom, bondage is getting left further and further behind.

Where the Spirit of the Lord is, there is freedom.

Little Foxes

"Catch all the foxes, those little foxes, before they ruin the vineyard, for the grapevines are blossoming" Song of Solomon 2:15.

In reading this, I was confused as to the reason they saw the foxes as a threat to their vineyard. I know foxes are secretive, crafty, opportunistic creatures who will take full advantage of dining in my chicken coop if an opportunity presents itself. Those of us who raise chickens must be diligent to check the enclosures for signs of burrowing, as the foxes will do, to gain entry.

Why a vineyard? Foxes do not eat grapes, right? Foxes will eat anything they can find. I have discovered foxes love grapes. That's a problem for the vineyard.

Foxes are nocturnal animals. While you are out tending the grapes, they are sleeping away in their burrow. The burrow they dug right in the middle of their favorite food source. Yep, under the precious vines. Not only are they eating the grapes, they are uprooting the plants. The roots the vines need for nourishment to produce the very fruit we want them to produce.

In the verse, they are talking about catching all the foxes when the blossoms are appearing. Before the fruit comes. The phrase "ruining" was understood in the Hebrew text to mean, corrupting or destroying. Vineyards are meant to produce one thing…grapes. The vines in bloom would never produce any fruit if the foxes were not removed.

In John 15, it tells us that God is the vine and we are the branches. The branches cannot survive without the vine. The branch's purpose is to bear fruit. Yet, we must remember, the fruit has to stay on the vine to its maturity.

So, in the spiritual sense, little foxes left unchecked will destroy the very fruit God is calling us to produce.

What are the "little foxes" in our lives?

Everything big, first started small.

It's the statements, "I know I shouldn't but" or the "Just this one time." "It's no big deal."

For me, countless times, I said, "It's only food, it's no big deal." Looking back, I can see "blossoms" being destroyed by my inability (or just burying my head in the sand) to recognized the "little foxes" digging up my roots. The binging that brought shame, embarrassment, withdrawal, and insecurity. What "fruit" that made it to some level of maturity was malnourished and small.

Many times, I would draw the line in the sand and declare, "NO MORE!" For a time, I would be successful in maintaining that line. A small choice, I am only going to eat one, would always lead to another then one day I would awake from the fog and ask "How did I get here? I was doing so well, what happened?" Little foxes left unchecked.

We have all heard "How do you eat an elephant? One bite at a

CHAPTER SIX - *LITTLE FOXES*

time." Here's the thing that the enemy knows when deploying his foxes against you. You will not notice the first few bites unless you are on the lookout for them. Even then it is easy to get caught off guard.

Remember every big thing started off small.

One decision. One step. One choice. One look.

We are told that broad is the way that leads to destruction and narrow is the way that leads to life. If you are flying from New York to Hong Kong but not using any instruments to keep you on course, you will not wind up in Hong Kong. No pilot would ever do that and you would never knowingly get on that plane.

How do I recognize the little foxes?

You must first be honest with yourself. Where are you being challenged? What is a trigger that leads you down the wide path?

Is there one thing that seems to catch you off guard?

For me, it comes back to food. That is the weapon of choice of the enemy for me. It is the one-degree course correction that left unchecked (or ignored) that will lead me off the proverbial cliff.

That "one thing" that "trigger" for me is refined carbs. Harmless, right? For me it's not. I now live in the gluten free world. My system does not like gluten, so I choose not to eat it. No, I do not push the boundaries, not because I have super hero willpower, it makes me miserable. I can't tell you how many times I have had people say, "I wish I had your willpower then I wouldn't eat chocolate or fill in the blank." No super willpower here. I know, there are a few things that are "allowed" on my diet that I will absolutely eat all of it in one sitting. Yes, they are allowed but should they be on my weekly menu? Nope! For me, eating refined carbs leads to eating more refined carbs and so on.

Here's the key for me. Boundaries. Just like I have to keep my eye on the fenced enclosure of my chickens for predator damage. I MUST keep track of my food boundary. If I do not track my refined carbs…yes, I mean write them down, before I can count to 5, I will be on a full-blown carb binge.

Proverbs 25:28 "A person without self-control is like a city with broken down walls."

I need walls!!!! There is protection, safety, and believe it or not, there is freedom within the walls.

That is how the little foxes got into the vineyard, there were no walls.

If I am not within my boundaries, then my roots are easily accessible to damage. My time outside the walls gets comfortable and soon, I will not even be aware that I am in trouble. That is how the enemy works. He wants you to become so comfortable with what is dangerous for you so you no longer recognize the danger. My husband told me a story that the key note speaker at a men's conference shared. A man had a snake, one he had no business having, a dangerous one like a constrictor or an anaconda. One day he was lying on his bed watching TV and he had this snake in the bed with him. It was acting different than normal. It was stretched full length and stiff. He called the vet because he was concerned. After hearing what was happening, the vet told him to slowly and quietly get out of the bed then leave the room and close the door behind him. It was then the vet explained that the snake was preparing to eat him. Laying full out next to him, measuring up to see if he would fit. That my friends is how the enemy works in our lives. So comfortable in the dangerous situation you no longer see the danger. That is how the little foxes destroy the vineyard and destroy the fruit you are wanting in your life.

Proverbs 14:1 "A wise woman builds her house, but a foolish one tears it down with her own hands."

Which one do I want to be?

It's not just with our eating habits. It's with all arenas of life. They are doing their silent, sneaky work on our character and the longer they are allowed to continue, the longer they have to dig up, and destroy the foundation of your faith.

Proverbs 1:7 "The fear of the Lord is the foundation of true knowledge."

Proverbs 27:12 "A prudent man foresees danger and takes precaution."

Our choices and actions affect others.

Let's look at Saul. He was chosen as king by God. How cool is that?! Yet, at the very beginning, we see his lack of faith in God and what God called him into. He was hiding so they would pass him by. God calls and Saul hid. Yes, he was still anointed as king. Many choices were made due to his lack of faith in his ability to do what God wanted as God wanted. He deferred to peoples wishes and wants. God, then chooses another to be king.

Now his army is facing down the Philistines again. Victory had been theirs in prior encounters. This time, the Philistines have a huge guy named Goliath. This time, Saul and his entire army forgot who they served and only saw the impossibility of defeating Goliath on their own. Saul's choice to not follow God is now permeating his troops. I picture each soldier looking at the guy next to him saying "You fight him." Saul's poor choices led to the erosion of faith within his entire army. Not one of them stood up to Goliath in the name of the Lord. Come on! They were the Lord's army!

I know, I am not a leader of an army but my choices affect my family. My sugar fixations were being broadcast to my kids. In order to break that cycle, I had to break of the choice.

Someone is always watching.

Not many begin gambling because they wanted to lose everyone and everything they care about.

How many well-known pastors have fallen into adultery and lost family and reputation.

Every big thing starts as a small thing.

It took one look for King David. He was where he was not supposed to be when he first saw Bathsheba. One look and it changed her life, her husband's life, David's life, and took the life of their firstborn son. One look seems harmless. We must look at the bigger picture. How will the vineyard look if I let this continue? What damage could occur?

Saul and his army faced off against Goliath for 40 days. Every morning and every evening, they would put on their battle gear and march to the frontlines. With shouts and battle cries they would line up, draw their weapons and stand ready. They went through the motions. They looked like they would do battle.

How often have I gone through the motions. Reading my daily devotionals, listening to worship music, and saying the right phrases. I am looking the part! I have even "put on" my armor and have my

CHAPTER SIX - *LITTLE FOXES*

shield. This is where the enemy wants us. Looking the part but without the foundation. Every building is built on a foundation. This is the core of how it stands. This is the very thing the enemy is after. He comes to destroy the foundation of Jesus Christ in our lives.

He does it through seemingly small, of no consequence, decisions. Remember Eve? He simply asked her a question that has altered every person's life since. Every. Single. One. Of. Us.

What little foxes are in your life?

- Little white lies.
- Poor financial choices.
- Looking at things on the computer that you know you shouldn't be.
- Gossip.
- Marital challenges.
- Drugs and or Alcohol.
- Binging on anything.
- Shopping.

Oh, the list of how he uses foxes against us in our lives is vast. He knows where we are weak and uses the weak spots to infiltrate.

How do we shore up our boundaries? Build the wall around your life.

Read the word of God. Remove that which is a trigger. I know that's a "duh" right. If you have a shopping problem, you shouldn't take your "shopping" buddy! You know you will buy both pairs of shoes!

In the book of Nehemiah, he is tasked with rebuilding the wall around Jerusalem. The wall was critical to the city's security. Not all were thrilled about this. They liked having Jerusalem wide open, an easy target. When the ones who wanted to stop the wall from being built came up against him, Nehemiah replied "I am doing a great work and cannot come down." The enemy will always send something to distract you to keep you off course. He wants you to lose focus and stop building. He wants you wide open and an easy target. It's time to stop giving the enemy what he wants. Nehemiah and the citizens rebuilt that wall in 52 days. Without heavy equipment or fancy tools. They defended themselves and each other and remained focused on the work. Attacks came and they still built.

"On Christ the solid rock I stand, all other ground is sinking sand."

Build the wall.

We can build the wall with solid rock or sand. The choice is ours.

Guarding your life, your home, and your family from the foxes the enemy sends, is doing a great work. Do not listen to the one who wants you to stop.

Stay the course. When you notice a course deviation, get back on the right course. Press into the One who loves you and wants to help you. If you are a follower of Jesus, you have the Holy Spirit that is your helper. Ask Him to help you and then LET Him!! Press through the minefield the enemy lays for you.

What foxes are eroding your foundation?

CHAPTER SIX - *LITTLE FOXES*

- Unforgiveness.
- Pride.
- Procrastination.
- Selfishness.
- Anger.
- Bitterness.
- Gossip.
- Lying.

There is nothing too big, to messed up, too far gone that God is unable nor unwilling to redeem.

You are loved more than you know. Jesus is waiting for you to turn back to Him. Give your whole list to him and watch what he can do. Do not wait. It's time to thrive in the vineyard.

Let us remove the little foxes before they ruin our life.

Mount Rushmore

Today as I was doing my morning workout routine, towards the end of this intense, "muscles dying" block of exercises. The instructor tells us, "I know it's hard, dig deep into your why, the why you are here, the why you are doing this and it will give you the strength to carry you through." I looked at her and said, "Nope, you are wrong." It wasn't actually to her face. I work out in my living room because the program I follow is online.

Knowing our "why" is all the rage in the coaching world right now. Know your why and you will succeed. Your why is your power. I do talk about the "why" with my clients. It brings clarity to the mission, but it is only part of the picture.

Remember in the movie *The Wizard of Oz*, how you were to pay no attention to the man behind the curtain? The wizard seemed all powerful with his booming voice and flashing lights. Everyone followed him because of what they saw and heard. When, in reality, the wizard was just an ordinary guy.

I think the enemy of our souls works a lot like that. He seems big and loud and powerful yet he works best hiding behind a distraction.

I think this focus on knowing our why is a distraction. Yes, it has really good meaning behind it but it takes the focus off the most important reason behind our decision. The why keeps us focused on self. What about me? What is good for me? Me. Me. Me. When the road that is inspired to take, because of the why, gets difficult to walk, we dig deep to keep on it but often decide this "why" isn't really needed for my life. The enemy knows that by ourselves, we are weak. He knows the why is not enough.

Remember that Satan goes about roaring like a lion, looking for one to devour! Just as a wolf pack will look for the prey by itself, so does our enemy. Distraction works. It takes our eyes focused on what is in it for me. Remember the question he asked Eve? Did God really say? He then talked about what this fruit would give her. He got her to take her eyes off all she was given and focus on the one she was not supposed to touch.

The enemy is on a mission. He wants to take as many people with him as he can to the lake of fire and he will use whatever he can to make it happen.

The distractions always have a bit of truth woven in or we would recognize the lie. He likes to make it sound good. "God helps those who help themselves." Sounds empowering, but it is not found in God's word. A distraction may sound empowering but 99% truth is still not truth. My husband liked to use this example when he was teaching, "I made this pan of brownies just for you, they are still warm from the oven and they smell amazing, anyone want one? Oh, and I put just a little dog poo in them but you won't taste it." Of course, all the girls screamed and the boys laughed. If it's not 100% truth it is not truth, a little bit of distraction, or diversion added to it and it becomes like the brownies.

So, if "why" isn't my power statement, what is?

I am so glad you asked!

Your true power, strength comes from knowing your "Who."

Who are you doing this for? Who are you living your life for? Who gives you strength? Who gives you life, hope, confidence, laughter, healing, and the list goes on.

Answer that and you are on the right path.

As for me, I have made the decision to lay my life down to Jesus. Surrender it all for Him. I want to be completely used up when I meet Him face to face because I held nothing back. As Jennie Allen says in her book, "Anything, Lord, I give you anything. Anything you ask, anything you want. I am yours for anything." When I first prayed that, all I could hear in my mind, "First count the cost." Enter the enemy's distraction technique, "that's too high of a cost." "He will move you to a remote area in Africa where they have huge spiders." Really, I will not say it has been easy or comfortable. I think the enemy wants me to stay in my comfortable.

So, we know the enemy comes to steal, kill, and destroy everything. Yes, I mean everything. Our hopes, dreams, families, homes, friendships, jobs, and the list keeps on going!

How are we to stand against him? In James, we are told to resist the devil and he will flee from you. Am I doing this wrong? He keeps coming back and catching me unaware. Distraction!

Of course, he will try again. Remember he is after taking you and everyone you care about to the lake of fire with him. He will use where he tripped you up before again and again and again.

So how do we fight against this seemingly huge mountain we are facing?

Mount Rushmore has the faces of 4 presidents carved on it and is one of National Parks. It was the brain child of the then governor as a way to attract more visitors to his state. It took 14 years, 200 hundred workers and tons of dynamite to get it to where we see it today. The artist commissioned to carve it died before it was finished and his son completed it.

The artist wanted the figures to be carved to their waist not just their faces. There were great discussions on who would be on the mountain. Custer was talked about and well as Sitting Bull. The presidents were chosen because of their significance to the country.

For the faces to be revealed in the mountain, stone had to be removed. No one traveling by the mountain prior to the work stopped and said "Look, I see George Washington's face."

When we lay our heart down to Jesus, we do not automatically reflect his image. We too are a work in progress and the finish product is not going to look like we thought it would. But, just like the reason behind the Mount Rushmore project, to attract people to the state. Our transformation draws others to Jesus.

This is why we must fight against the enemy. This is why he wants to stop the work the Holy Spirit does within us.

Okay, the enemy has 3 outcomes he is after. Kill, steal, and destroy. He uses distraction to get us off focus. He also has in his arsenal, what I call "the triplets." Fear. Doubt. Worry. He wields these well.

In Psalm 91: 2 "This, I will declare about the Lord: He alone is my refuge, my place of safety: he is my God and I trust him."

God knows what the enemy is up too. In Job 1, Satan had to ask God for his permission to mess with Job. God knows what the enemy is doing, how he fights and what we need to withstand the attack.

In Ephesians 6: 11 "Put on all of God's armor so that you will be able to stand firm against all strategies of the devil."

God's armor fits. Let's get dressed!

Helmet of Salvation

Oh, how the enemy loves to mess with our minds! He plants fear deep in the "I am not good enough" "I will lose everything" "I can never be forgiven." He distorts God's truth. He condemns. He distracts. He flat out lies.

We need the helmet to filter everything through. He brings condemnation when I fall off the food truck and go on a binge. I can choose to listen to him or I can choose to rebuke him with the truth of God's word. Jesus offers forgiveness, healing, and strength to get back up again and stand.

We need the helmet when the enemy says that God will never forgive us for the choices we made. The abortion, drug addictions, adultery, and pornography. He asks us how we can ever forgive ourselves for these choices. The Word tells us that anyone who is in Christ is a new creation, the old is gone. That God removes our sins as far as the east is from the west and remembers them no more. We need to get excited about that!

The helmet is our "truth filter." Put it on! Quit listening to the enemy!

Belt of Truth

Oh boy, do we need this! Remember how the enemy likes to distract us from the whole truth. The belt is amazing, it was the last piece of the armor for the Roman soldiers. It held the rest of the armor in place. Truth. Jesus said, I AM the Way, the Truth and the Life. Jesus is truth. Anything less than truth is not Jesus.

When Satan comes slithering over to talk to you and says, "Did God really say?" He wants you to doubt, he wants you to second guess the truth. Do not engage in a conversation with him like Eve did. In John 8:31-32 Jesus said, "You are truly my disciples if you remain faithful to my teachings. Then you will know the truth and the truth will set you free." Remain in Jesus and his teachings and you will know the truth.

Breastplate

This piece covers your vital organs, it protects your heart. The word tells us that our heart is deceitful above all else. Its natural bent is deceit. Imagine what it would look like if we let the enemy in. Guard your heart. What we let in will take root. The fruit of the spirit, love, joy, peace, patience, kindness, goodness, gentleness, and self control. Oh, what would my heart could look like! Or the flip side, unforgiveness, bitterness, pride, rejection, and strife. The enemy is after your heart to destroy it. Jesus wants to redeem it.

Shoes

The Roman soldier's sandals had spikes on the soles to give them a firm grip and to keep them from slipping. God gives us shoes to wear that are the peace that comes from the gospel. We are to stand firm in the shoes of the peace (which passes all understanding) of the Gospel of Jesus Christ. Peace, how our world needs such peace.

Satan has spread the opposite of peace in our lives. How often have I played the "worry about everything" game. What if this happens, what if it doesn't happen. I remember my grandma was always worrying about something. I think she would worry if she didn't have something to worry about. I have heard it said the worry is payment on a debt that is not due. Just like that enemy, keeping us distracted worrying about something we can do nothing about. Worry takes our focus off the One who can and puts it on us, who by ourselves cannot.

Shield of Faith

I love shields! The Roman soldiers shield was long enough and wide enough for them to hide completely behind. I can just picture an epic battle scene, watching them plant their shield using it to take the hits from the enemy while they fire back from a place of safety. The shield of faith. Faith, the confidence of what we hope for and the assurance about what we do not see. Hebrews 11:1.

The assurance of what we hope for. Who is our hope? Jesus Christ. The shield of faith is faith in the reality of who Jesus is. Our confidence is in Him and our assurance of His promise.

Here the enemy comes and sows doubt. You don't have enough faith, if you did the outcome would be different. If you truly had faith you would be…

A dear woman from church passed, she was so well loved. Her faith was unwavering through the battle. Her 4 words, will I pray, help you through the battle you are facing. "I am trusting God."

That's faith, the confidence of what we hope for and the assurance of what we cannot see.

Sword of the Spirit

Ephesians 6:17b "take the sword of the Spirt, which is the word of God."

In Matthew 4:1-11 the enemy came against Jesus 3 times in the wilderness. Jesus had been there for 40 days, fasting and he was hungry. He was weak and vulnerable, or so the enemy thought.

Three times he attempted to distract Jesus from his purpose. Three times he came at him in his "weak" places. First temptation he tried was fleshly desires. We all recognize this one. "If it feels good, do it." Come on, Jesus was hungry! Yes, he was fully God but he was fully man and man needs to eat! He tried using his version of scripture to get him to cave. Then he tried one that works so well in our world today, the temptation of social position. Look what all you can have! It looks good!

How did Jesus stand? He resisted the devil with the Word of God.

We must know the word, not just sort of, maybe a little bit of, well I am not so good at memorizing it, does not make the enemy flee.

I am guilty of declaring "I am not good at memorizing scripture." Words have such power. I really became terrible at memorizing. Self-fulfilling…here's the truth, when we hide the word in our heart, the Holy Spirit will bring them to mind for us to use against the enemy. If I do not hide them in my heart they will not be there when I need them. If I am not in the word, how can I hide it in my heart?

Matthew 4: 11 "Then the devil went away, and the angels came and took care of Jesus."

I love this picture. After the battle, Jesus is ministered too. When we are weary from the fight, who is right there with us? Jesus and the Holy Spirit.

In the process of breaking free from addictive patterns, I have experienced all these tactics of the enemy. Many times, it seemed as if the mountain was just too large and it was hopeless. I fought against

Fear

I would never be free.

Doubt

I wouldn't be successful.

Worry

What happens when I fall down and mess things up? What will others think of me?

This is how the enemy operates. I was so addicted to chocolate that I couldn't see how I could possibly live without it. It sounds silly when I write it but that was my reality. I had tried many times. Failed just as many. Even though chocolate was making me physically miserable, I still was unable to break free.

It was in my desperation that God moved. When I reached the end of me and my strength. Sitting in a rest stop, tears streaming down my face, I said, "God I cannot do this!" I heard a voice as clear as if someone was sitting next to me in my car, "I can." I turned it all over to God right there and He did.

I would love to be able to tell you that is how he works every time for everyone in every situation, but it's not. I thought I was so together. I conquered chocolate! I am saved! Where was the recognition of God for what He did for me? Distractions are real and he used them to keep my eyes on me. With my focus on me and what I had accomplished, I was an easy target for the enemy. I let the enemy take me down other paths of addictive patterns. Off all chocolate, sugar became my food of choice. All sugar. The more I had, the more I wanted. Never realizing it was a problem. Chocolate was obvious- it gave me huge hives and I was miserable. Sugar, no problem here, nothing to see here, I'm just hanging out with my buddy, sugar.

Until the day of reckoning came. Yes, they come.

Again, I was desperate. I cried out to God. This time there was no voice to be heard. Just a knowing deep within me that I had to move forward. I felt like one of the Hebrews, stuck between the Red Sea and the entire Egyptian army.

This time the road to freedom was hard! I battled headaches, tiredness, CRABBINESS, and so many other withdrawal symptoms. I have since discovered that sugar is considered one of the most addictive substances. I am not comparing addictions. All of them are a hard-fought battle to freedom.

The enemy likes to drag me back in to the sugar bowl and play a few rounds. Sometimes, I am strong, wearing my armor and aware of what he is trying to do. Other times, his distractions are successful and I find myself head first in to the sugar bowl.

I know what freedom feels like and I know the battle it takes to get there.

Fight for your freedom my friend.

Chasing Perfection

I am in the dressing room, holding up this pair of jeans. Thinking, "Are these going to fit?" They are the size I normally wear but I am feeling a little "swollen" today. Well, here it goes. I cannot even get them all the way up. No matter how much I do the "putting on tight jeans" dance, they are not budging. I catch my reflection in the mirror and scowl. Look at me, fat bulging, stomach hanging out, what is wrong with me. I never should have had that dessert. Uhggg, I am just so fat. As I am peeling them off, I hear my husband ask, "Are you going to let me see them?" Gosh, I forgot he was here. Now what do I do? I put a smile on my face and peek out the curtain. Calmly telling him that the jeans just didn't work. Then it happened, the statement that no woman ever wants to hear her husband say, "Do you need a bigger size? I can get it for you."

My husband is thinking how he can help me. He wants to solve my problem. Do I need a bigger size?

I am, however, mortified, crushed, and vowing he will never see me naked again. I didn't realize he thought I was fat. Why didn't he tell me he thinks I am fat? Well, probably because he would be dead. He wants me to get the next bigger size, now I am angry. Yeah, there is "angry" going on. Angry at myself because the jeans didn't fit. Angry because I don't like how I feel about myself because they didn't fit and angry because my husband agrees with those soul crushing jeans that didn't fit. Oh, and one more angry, he wants to "help me" by reminding me that the jeans didn't fit.

He is clueless as to why I am upset. Clueless as to why I am saying, "I'm fine" over and over again. He is like a deer in the headlights, knows he is in danger of being hit but not sure where to move to! Even if he did get the other jeans and I tried them on (not happening!) I am sure as Jesus is Lord, I am not buying them. That would be a confirmation that the first soul sucking pair of jeans were right, I am fat and my husband thinks so too.

Craziness right? Why do we give such power to a little tag on our clothes? Really, the size tag makes up less than 1% of the article of clothing yet we let it dictate how it makes us feel about ourselves.

Here's the truth about the fashion industry. We know there is no uniformity in the sizes of clothing for women. What is labeled as a small in one brand would be considered a large in another. The same confusion exists in our entire wardrobe.

Here is how I see it. The enemy designs women's clothing. He is the author of confusion. He wants to rob us of our peace so he plays clothing size roulette. He wins the game and we keep placing the marble on a number, hoping we get lucky.

We go up a size - we feel like a failure, fat, ugly, lazy, shame, rejection, and did I say ugly? Yeah, let's listen to the enemy tell us that one more time. "You are ugly!" No one thinks you are beautiful and they all notice your clothes seem tight.

We go down a size - we win self-love, confidence, acceptance, we share the news with friends and celebrate, feel beautiful, happy,

CHAPTER EIGHT - *CHASING PERFECTION*

and in control. Oh, and new clothes, gotta have new clothes with a new number on them.

We drop a size, lose some weight, and we walk different. You know it's true! We walk like we are taller. Heads held high, shoulders back, no reason to slump anymore. We feel so confident, we smile at everyone, and we feel beautiful.

We celebrate with our friends who lose weight. We should because that was hard work getting to their goal. We tell them "You look beautiful!," "You look amazing!," "You look better than you did in high school." Our comments are based on how they look. So, my question is this, were they not beautiful before?

Were they not amazing already? Of course they were! But in our cultural perception, small is to be desired, admired, and praised. But only when it pertains to a number on a scale or on a clothing label. Every other area of our lives we chase big, bigger house, bigger bank account, corner office, 401k's, paychecks, followers on social media, bigger cars, vacations, social status, careers, degrees…chasing big as if big is all that is important.

I have chased a number on the scale for the past 40 years. Frankly, I am exhausted. I have come to realize that a number is just a thing. It doesn't define who I am. It has no power to make me a better person, better wife, mother, or make Jesus love me less or more. The only power it has is what I give it. I refuse to waste anymore of my time bowing at the altar of the scale or living my life for the approval of a tag on my clothes.

My battle with the scale began at 15. I was playing softball and was moved to catcher. I normally played in the outfield so this was a huge change. I really was not good at it! Having missed several balls that required me chasing after them, I heard a woman in the stands remark, "That's good, she is rather chubby, she needs the exercise." I had never even thought about my weight. I just ate what I wanted and wore what fit. That freedom ended, crashed head first into a brick wall. I stepped on the scale and chose a number that I thought sounded the opposite of chubby and stopped eating.

Chasing that number (which, by the way, was totally unrealistic, only children weigh that!) has caused me so many tears. I had it in my head that reaching that number would make me perfect, accepted, and beautiful. I was chasing perfection at the expense of my health, my mental well-being, relationships, and I was willing to get it at any cost.

Chasing perfection is like trying to catch the wind that blows in every direction.

Perfection (noun) - The condition, state, or quality of being free or as free as possible from all flaws or defects. The action or process of improving something until it is as faultless as possible.

Whose idea of perfection are we chasing? Hollywood's portrayal of the perfect woman? The fashion industry standard for what size a woman must be? The sitcom wife, who works full-time while going to school, raising 3 kids, and her house is always immaculate? The "reality" show seeking her perfect man?

We say things like, "My steak is cooked to perfection." When Gordan Ramsey says this, I know it's a beautiful medium rare. That is not perfection for me. I would make a face at how red it still is and declare it to still be mooing! Clearly, we view perfection differently.

The perfect vacation. Close your eyes and imagine yours. For some it would be in a tropical location, an exotic destination, a romantic cruise, hiking in the wilderness or staying at home.

CHAPTER EIGHT - *CHASING PERFECTION*

Babe Ruth is one of the greatest baseball players of all time. His record of 60 home runs in a season stood for 30 years. His batting average was .342. Doing some research on the average baseball average, I discovered the highest league batting average was in 1930 which was .296. These athletes are paid big money for their skill. Yet, they, who are considered some of the best, miss more than they get a hit.

Whose work is perfect? Picasso or Mozart?

Sit with me here for a moment. Are you thinking that because they are different examples of artistic expression we are unable to compare them?

Yes, we can, and we do it every day.

Every time I compare myself to another person.

Every time I compare someone's talent with another's.

Every time I look at one's size and declare a judgment based on my opinion of what size they should be.

Every time I judge my life based on what I think I see in someone else's.

We compare Mozart to Picasso all day long. Both were masters in their field. Both are highly regarded yet neither could fill in for the other.

You are the only you.

Chasing perfection creates a vacuum in our soul that will never be satisfied.

Perfect, there is only one who was and is perfect, Jesus Christ.

The only one without sin became sin and died for each one of us so we may be free from the stain of our choice.

In the beginning, God created the heavens and the earth. Each day he expanded his work and at the end of each day, he declared it good. He then placed Adam and Eve into the garden, the perfect place to be. They made a bad decision and their life in the garden ended. Sin entered the world and it has never been the same.

We still see indescribable beauty. The brilliant sunsets, a newborn child, flowers in bloom, the stars in the night sky, and the love that fills our hearts.

All of us are drawn to beauty. All of us see beauty, just not in the same things nor in the same ways.

We are created in his image. We are beautiful. Yes, each and every one of us, not one of us look exactly the same. All of us with our own "flaws" that we wish were gone.

When we strive for an idea of perfection- always seeking to reach it, we miss out on experiencing God's grace and provision in the "imperfect."

Peter, trying to be the perfect disciple boldly declares that he will never deny Jesus, even if all the others do. I bet he was thinking he had it all together! He did deny Jesus just as Jesus said he would. It broke his heart and he went back to fishing. Peter thought because he was wrong (AKA "not perfect"), it disqualified him. Jesus shows up and invites him to join him. Jesus asks Peter 3 times, "Do you love me?" Peter replies, Lord you know I do. His mission from Jesus was given to him after his fall. It was in Peter's dealing with his mistake (his imperfect action) that Jesus shows up. If Peter had not fallen, would his heart been truly ready to receive what Jesus

CHAPTER EIGHT - *CHASING PERFECTION*

was asking him to do? He knew what it felt like to deny Jesus to men and he would never do that again. It would ultimately cost him his life.

Paul was on the forefront of persecuting Christians. He was celebrated for his role in it. He even said he was the perfect Jew, "The Jew among Jews." He had done everything right, he had the right upbringing, the right education, and connections. Then he encountered Jesus, lost his vision for 3 days and became the one who would take the message to the Gentiles. He discovered what he had been building his life on, the rules, the status, were nothing. To live for Jesus was all he needed.

At a family gathering, a volley ball game was set up. I was asked to play but didn't. I knew I would not be good at it so I didn't play. Sidelined, watching others laugh at their missed hits, I felt envious. How is it they can be comfortable playing when they are not any good at it? They just jumping in, saying "I want to play," not getting bogged down by the "I don't know how and I will look foolish."

In the midst of growing up with a speech problem, I decided to never do anything that could get me laughed at. I had been laughed at enough and I was done. Playing it safe within my comfort zone of skill, the perfect place to be if I didn't want to be laughed at. Nothing good grows within our comfort zone. How do I grow into the woman God created me to be if I am not willing to step outside and try something new? I was stuck. Perfection was my prison and I had locked the door myself.

I think this is why Jesus said we must come to him as little children. Children naturally try new things. They learn to roll over, crawl, talk, walk, and then run. They are free from the burden of being perfect that we, as adults, place on ourselves. They take life head on, full of hope, and full of energy. They freely say, I will do it for any game, task or problem that comes their way. Our daughter's nickname when she was little was "Tori-do" because that was her response to everything she faced. Tori-do. She wanted to do it, she wanted to figure it out and do it.

I wonder if God had not instilled the mastery of these motor skills in us as babies, if we would be doing them now. I think it was necessary for us to learn them before we discovered it would be hard to learn. That we would fall down, make mistakes, learn it at a different pace than others, and not get it right the first time we tried. We would have to get up again and again.

In our quest for perfection, we get stuck at the starting line. We are stuck in the not knowing how to. That first step seems impossible, so we stay at the starting line, wishing we could get to the place we would feel comfortable in the race. The only way is to take a step. I met Tiger Woods years ago when he first came on the golf scene. Truthfully, I didn't know who he was. There was another employee that knew all about him. He admired his skill, and his accomplishments. I remember him stating that he wished he could play like Tiger. I, being golf naive, asked him why he thought he couldn't. His reply, "I would have to work too hard." He was at the starting line but chose not to walk the path necessary to get to the finish line he wanted.

We are called to move, to be transformed, to make disciples, and to love the Lord with all of our heart, soul, mind, and strength. None of which is just downloaded into us. We need to grow into who God created us to be. If we do not get that, we will never fulfill what He called us to do.

So today, start. Start exploring what God has placed in your

CHAPTER EIGHT - *CHASING PERFECTION*

heart. Ask yourself, "What makes you smile?," "What brings you joy?," "What brings tears to your eyes?," "Where do you want to sow God's love?," "Who needs to hear your story?"

You are here, at this time, for a reason. It is time for you to start living in the space of "his grace is sufficient for you." Start giving yourself some grace in your learning. Let go of the perfection illusion. Not one of us starts at the end and have all the knowledge, we all start at the beginning.

Discover you, incredible "beautifully imperfect" you.

Who Are You Looking At?

I was mindlessly scrolling through Facebook when I saw an ad pop up. It was promoting a creative bible journaling class in my area. What on earth is creative bible journaling? That was a new one for me. I thought it would be fun so I signed up and bought the Inspire bible they recommended.

Walking into the event I realized I was out of my element! There were assortments of coloring options on every table along with stickers, embellishments (I learned about them there, that's how I know what they are), and various ribbons. I remember thinking, "What have I gotten myself into?"

The speaker/instructor asked how many have done this before and 95% of the room raised their hands. I was thinking, it will be fine, I will be okay, maybe the women at my table with their hands raised can help me. Then it happened, the speaker lifted up her bible to show us how wonderful this creative journaling can be. I looked like a deer in the headlights. There were ribbons hanging out, she had jewels and beads, stickers and verse inspired drawings that looked like they should be framed. I was frozen, not sure if from shock or fear. All the others at my table were gleefully discussing what they were going to do with the page we were given. I was in a foreign land, trapped behind enemy lines. I wanted to pick up my bible and leave.

I picked up a marker trying to remember what she had told us. Trying to find some artistic inspiration, I glanced at the other work at my table. I was a kindergartner amongst the masters.

Lord, I am NOT creative! I am not like them. Why am I here?

So much happened within me in that very uncomfortable space.

God is the creator of everything. Everything! God is creative.

Yes, but - Wait I am created in Your image, that means I am creative also. No, I am not. Look at what these women are creating. I am not like them.

Who was I looking at, comparing myself to? My own God given talents and abilities to?

But - Hang on God, let me explain how I see it.

I am not - while pointing out what HE didn't give me, just so you know God.

Like - comparing to someone else to see how I measure up - to be like them. Showing how I am lacking because of what, in my opinion, God didn't give me.

This is all swirling in my heart, mind, and soul while I am trying to do something beautiful with this coloring project, she started us on.

"Them," that all-encompassing group of perfect people. Lifting them up to a place where they do not belong. I truly was coveting their creative talents. I was comparing myself to them and all I could

CHAPTER NINE - WHO ARE YOU LOOKING AT?

see was how I fell so short

When we compare - we lose.

Who was I looking at? Not God. I was grumbling about my shortcomings. I was afraid of what they would think of me. I was placing their opinion of me higher than what God says about me.

In Galatians 6:11-12 Paul writes, "NOTICE WHAT LARGE LETTERS I USE AS I WRITE THESE CLOSING WORDS IN MY OWN HANDWRITING. Those who are trying to force you to be circumcised want to look good to others. They don't want to be persecuted for teaching the cross of Christ alone can save."

This is important, so read it again!

When others, or yourself, push you into becoming just like someone else.

- Follow Jesus, just how they do.
- Follow these traditions
- Sing only these songs
- Read only this translation
- Pray only like this
- Dress just like this
- Look like them

WE MUST STOP!

We are never called to be just like someone else.

In verse 14 Paul said he never boasts about anything except the cross of Jesus Christ.

What we should be doing is taking our eyes off "them" and put it squarely on Jesus. It is in him that we are being transformed into a new creation.

Comparison runs rampant throughout our culture. We are the most marketed to people ever. We are exposed to ads 4,000 to 10,000 times daily (estimate is from 2015!). What car we should drive, the clothes we need to be wearing, what our house should look like, the jewelry we must have, the people we need to follow, the celebrities we should look up to, the gadget that will make our life easier, what we must look like to be beautiful, and the crazy list keeps going. It is insane. No car, jewelry or house is going to make me into someone else. Why am I caught in the trap of how they want to live?

The enemy is great at bringing to our attention what we do not have. Look how he got to Eve. He holds up the bright and shiny and tells us that if we only had this, then we would be happy. If only I sang like Carrie, played golf like Tiger, athletic like Shaq, smart like Einstein, tiny like Angelina or rich like Bill then I would be happy. Comparisons keep us chasing the "if I had, then I would," "If I looked like, then I would be." Remember, the enemy comes to lie, kill, steal, and destroy and yes, he is good at it.

As I began working on my page, I was listening to the conversations taking place. The conversations that happen when a group of women get together are amazing! I began to hear, "I love how you did that," "Teach me how you," "I can never get this part right," "You make it look so easy," "I messed this up so bad," "Don't look at mine, it's not good." I put down my marker and smiled. I thanked the Holy Spirit for showing me that I am not the only one

CHAPTER NINE - *WHO ARE YOU LOOKING AT?*

in the room is not confident in their ability to create. Sure, there are some more gifted, more practiced than others. Yet, it seemed as if each one was not sure how their work would measure up.

One of the hosts of the event went around to each table to check in, to offer advice, and encouragement. When she arrived at our table, she had many wonderful things to say to the other women. All of them had prior experience in this world of bible journaling and their work reflected that. She looked at mine, I could see it on her face, she really didn't know what to say. I smiled and told her I was enjoying myself and thanked her for doing this event. I am sure mine looked when, compared to the others at the table, like a 1st graders art project that you would put on your refrigerator. She smiled back at me and said, "Nice try."

A short time earlier, that comment would have hurt my feelings. I would have been embarrassed to show her what I had accomplished and probably given many excuses for it.

In my heart, I knew her comment to be true. It was a nice try. I had wandered into uncharted territory, unfamiliar with the process, tools, well everything and was creating something.

I picked up a few stickers and embellishments and did something with them.

Did it look like anyone else's? Nope, sure did not. I am 100% okay with that.

On the drive home, I asked God what He wanted me to learn from this night and what did he want me to do with it.

Stepping into "new" is difficult. We are unsure and feel as if we are lost.

We want to learn something. Let's just pick tennis. We find an instructor and sign up for lessons. Halfway through our first lesson, we have lost our enthusiasm and are frustration reigns because we expected to play like Serena Williams and we have not managed to get one ball over the net. We wonder who is watching us and what do they think.

Remember the movie Karate Kid? I love the scene where Mr. Miyagi had him wax his car and paint the fence. Wax on…wax off. He didn't understand how this would help him learn karate. In frustration, he called it quits. Only then, when confronted, did he see how every little activity he did taught him the moves he needed to learn.

New means it is unfamiliar. Being a new follower of Jesus is the same. Many feel that because they have surrendered their heart to Jesus, their life should be different. Well, it is but the transformation takes a life time. Our fleshly desires do not go quietly into the night. It takes time. We all begin at the beginning. Give yourself the grace God does and keep trying.

We compare ourselves to an "expert" and feel like we fall so short that we shouldn't bother with trying.

I think we all have the "perfect" woman in our church, family, friend or work. You know the one who looks as if she has it all together and secretly you wish you were like her. A few years ago, we were experiencing major battles in our house. The enemy was pounding on us and our kids. At that time, I felt as if the enemy had taken more ground than we had gained. It was rough. After one service, our pastor had those in leadership go to the front of the church to pray for those who needed it. I went but I honestly felt so beat up I didn't think I had much to offer. One woman came forward for prayer. She told me that she wanted prayer for her family. She said she knew I wouldn't understand because my family was perfect. Perfect. Oh, we are so far from it. She had no idea the warfare going on in our house or the despair in my heart, or that my knees felt bloody from prayer. She thought she knew all about me because of how she saw me. We are all going through something. Yes, even those who you think have it all together. Most struggles and scars are not visible to the public. We compare based on our opinion, which is based on what we think we see and we rarely see the whole picture.

We focus on our lack of ability instead of relaxing and giving ourselves the space and grace to learn this new thing.

This is all I could see when I began the creative journaling class. What I couldn't do, what talent I didn't have. How many times in my life has this stopped me from trying something I wanted to try. I was afraid of looking foolish, being laughed at. The first time I was asked to be part of the *Unlocking Your Inner Warrior* book series, I said no. I am not an author. I am NOT like Beth Moore or Joyce Meyer. How can I let anyone read what I have written. What if they don't like it. What if it's terrible. What if. What if. Listening to the "what if's" kills more dreams than our enemy ever did.

I was blessed with an incredible editor who patiently corrected my grammar and work diligently to know my voice so it still could be heard within my writing, and a publisher who knew how to guide me. I was given the grace and space from those who knew to grow into the realization that "I am an author." If only my kindergarten teacher could see me now!

We look at what we accomplish as trivial and unimportant.

I hear this in every one of my small groups. In every one, there is at least one woman who qualifies her answer with, "This probably isn't right but this is how I answered it." Or "I just do not know as much as you." It breaks my heart. I certainly do not have all the answers, no one does. We are told "do not look down on anyone because they are young," yet we look down on ourselves when we think we do not measure up to someone or we are not as good at something. We withhold due to lack of confidence in ourselves. We listen to the enemy whisper that we will look foolish, sound stupid or the one that worked on me, they will laugh at you. I spent too many of my years hiding because I refused to put myself in a place where it was possible to be laughed at. I had enough of that growing up with a speech problem. If I never stood out, no one would notice me and if no one noticed, there could never be laughter.

When my first book was released, I was excited and terrified. Mostly terrified. I was "qualifying" how I told people about it. It's my first one. I have never done anything like this before. My part is okay but the rest is amazing. Then an amazing thing happened. The book went #1 new release on amazon. What?!

When I told people, I was wondering if they thought I was bragging. So, I stopped talking about it.

I have since recognized the enemy's tactics in this. I have been part of 4 other best sellers. I am excited how people's lives have been impacted by what I shared. I love hearing their stories. I have learned not everyone is going to like what you do. That is why there are thousands of weight loss programs, workout programs, hair salons, clothing lines, and shoes. Not one is necessarily better than the others, they just appeal to different people. Not everything works for everyone. I cannot be, nor expected too, be accepted by everyone. Neither will you. Become the person God created you to be anyway! There is one who sticks by you through everything. He

CHAPTER NINE - *WHO ARE YOU LOOKING AT?*

will never leave you nor forsake you. He is your strength, refuge, redeemer, and savior. That my friend is the greatest accomplishment of all. There is nothing trivial about your relationship with Jesus.

One of the greatest takeaways from my creative journaling class was that I realized I spent too much time and energy comparing my beginnings with other people's journey who are further down the road. I allowed the enemy to twist this habit for his good. I let myself be trapped in a "I am never good enough" prison. I decorated the walls with all the things that I thought I was lacking so I could look at them all day long. Then I discovered I held the key.

The time to stop listening to the enemy is now.

How do I recognize the difference between God's voice and the voice of the enemy?

God's voice: He speaks through scripture. You must spend time reading the word. I love listening to it doing daily tasks. He brings conviction, direction, healing, hope, love, forgiveness, and restoration.

The enemy always condemns, destroys, distracts, and divides. His words never line up against scripture. He uses our thoughts against us which is why we are told that we must take every thought captive.

Who are you listening to? Listen to the one who gave everything for you. Jesus would have gone to the cross even if you were the only one. He did this for you.

The world does not need another _____. You can fill this in with any name you want. It doesn't matter. The world already has a _____. The world needs you to flourish being you.

Look to the one who created you. He calls you his own. He calls you by name.

The Fairest

Sitting here, staring at the computer screen, listening to the second hand of my clock tick. When I first laid out this book and all of the chapters, this chapter, The Fairest, was the one I was most excited to write. I was eager to regale you with Psalm 139 and how you are fearfully and wonderfully made. How you are created in God's image, He is beautiful so you are too. Yet, every time I begin to write, all I hear is the second hand on my clock. With each tick, I am being reminded of the approaching deadline and there is far more to being called the Fairest than I realized.

In a previous chapter, Mirror Mirror, we saw the queen desperate to be known as the most, without comparison, and without rival. The familiar road she took to obtain it, cost her everything.

As I am writing this, I am fighting a cold. Wrapped in a big sweater with hot tea and tissues by my side. Sleepless nights due to difficulty breathing have brought the paleness and dark circles that highlight my face. My voice sounds like an ancient grizzly bear and my nose rivals Rudolph's. Just a glimpse behind the scenes of what I thought this was all about. Fairest? Not today, not by a long shot. Scariest? That's more accurate. My outward appearance clearly shows the physical distress I am under. Going out like this?

You mean in public? To be seen by anyone? Not going to happen.

I can only imagine what it is like to live under constant scrutiny. I think it would be like living in a glass house, knowing there are people right outside ready to take your picture, display it, with their opinion about your look, for the whole world to see. All of the opinions on how you look, what you wear, your relationships, your work, what they would do if they were you, and whatever else they can dream up to talk about. All this opinion madness fuels the sports talk radio and entertainment/gossip magazines. No good mistake can go left untalked about. We seem to eat it up! No thank you. I am hard enough on myself without having a group of people telling me how messed up they think I am.

So, what does the "Fairest" standard look like?

In the book of Matthew, we are introduced to John the Baptist. His clothes were woven from coarse camel hair and he ate locusts. I am thinking he looked something like a wild man. Not sure how many churches would heartily welcome him in to preach on Sunday morning. Certainly not when it's on live stream. How many of us form an opinion of someone based on how they look?

Why we dress the way we do. What others are wearing. What they look like. Truth moment here…Ladies we dress for the other women that will be there. Come on you know it's true!

How many fashion blogs are there telling us how we should be dressing? Exercise videos that tell us how to have the perfect body. Diet programs telling us what to eat and when to eat. What car we need to be driving to be noticed. Entertainment news and magazines to keep us up to date with the latest gossip.

We are bombarded by the unrelenting voices telling us what we

CHAPTER TEN - *THE FAIREST*

must heed these opinions to be valued.

Can we just take a pause?

Step back?

Turn off the noise!

Get down on our knees and be quiet.

Are we open to hearing the One's opinion that truly matters?

As I have been working on this book, I have found myself just staring at this title, The Fairest.

What does it mean?

Who is it?

Do I believe it?

How do I know it's true?

What does God say about me?

What does God say about Himself?

How can I help another asking these same questions?

I thought this was about us discovering that we are "the fairest." I was caught in the small. Worried about the mirror, the scale, others opinions, surviving without chocolate, a size, a look, being accepted, and placing all of the above before what comes first. It was like I was wandering in the desert chasing the mirage. So thirsty, crawling across the sand, thinking, "the water is right there, if I can just get there, then I'll be happy, pretty, accepted, noticed, and a thousand other words we can put in here." We do this in every area of our life.

- Our weight.
- Our identity.
- Our relationships.
- Our career.
- Our kids.
- Our finances.

When will I ever be enough?

Does God even notice me?

I was hoping for water but instead got a mouthful of sand of regret, disappointment, and shame.

In the book of Esther, she was chosen because of her outward appearance. I look in the mirror and see one who would have been passed by, wouldn't have made the cut in the search for beauty. Stuck in the outward focus, judging how I look compared to another, complaining to God that I got the "short straw." All I have to do is look at *People Magazine's* "Most Beautiful" for confirmation. In 1 Samuel 16:7, we are told that WE judge based on the outward but God looks at the heart.

What does my heart look like? All about me, truthfully.

What does God's heart look like?

John 3:16 "For God so loved the world, He gave so we could be free."

Psalm 23:6 "His good and unfailing love pursues me all the days of my life."

CHAPTER TEN - *THE FAIREST*

Psalm 139:17 "How precious are your thoughts about me, O God. They cannot be numbered."

Isaiah 43: "Do not be afraid, for I have ransomed you. I have called you by name and you are mine."

John 15:16 "You did not choose me. I chose you."

Galatians 1:15 "Before I was born, God chose me and called me by his marvelous grace."

Chosen. Sit here for a moment. You are chosen. Not because of what you did, how you look, or how popular you are. Not for being picked for a team based on how good you are. Standing there until the last few, hoping you won't be picked last again. Knowing they didn't want you, they were stuck with you.

You are chosen by the One who created it all.

The very One who spoke and everything was. Psalm 33:6-7. The One who calls the stars by name, created the universe, knows the very number of grains of sand, knit you together in your mother's womb, and the hair on your head. That One who calls you chosen.

That's often challenging to wrap my brain around. How can I possibly ever hope to live up to that? I make so many mistakes and my mouth often gets me into trouble (where is that holy duct tape when I need it?). He knows everything about me so why would he want me?

In Song of Songs 1:5-6, she declares, "I am dark but lovely." This one verse gave me a new understanding of how God sees me. I focus on the dark. My mess-ups, sins, habits, words, actions, well, all the stuff I do that I know I shouldn't do. I thought that my past sins were always before me. Ready to parade themselves out for

God to judge me on again and again and again. As if I was on a merry go round ride that never ended. It was in this "dark" I saw my identity. No amount of scrubbing could ever make it go away. Permanently stained for the whole world to see. That, my friends, is how the enemy kept me in bondage for years! So, when I read this verse for the first time, I was speechless. How can one be dark and lovely at the same time?

Revelation 3:20 "Behold I stand at the door and knock. If anyone hears my voice and opens the door, I will come in and dine with him, and he with Me."

Jesus, the One who gave it all, stands at the door of our hearts and knocks. He never barges in. He stands there knocking on the door of our heart, waiting for us to open our heart to Him.

Here's the thing, I was really good at opening the door for a quick peek and then shutting it. Trying to get enough Jesus in that moment but still hiding in the dark from him. I knew I needed something but was so sure I was no longer eligible to receive it and it would be forever out of my reach. I'm telling you, the dark stayed, camped out, and tattooed itself to my heart. I lived in fear of what God was going to do to me to repay me for what I had done. You know the "eye for an eye."

We were expecting our first child. I walked on eggshells, waiting for the "other shoe to drop." I had aborted my first baby years before and fully expected God to take this one in retaliation. That is what I deserved. I had an easy pregnancy and a not so easy delivery. I remember when they handed me our son for the first time and told me he was perfect. Perfect? Really? Are they sure? I didn't understand what was happening. When my mom came into the room to see us, she saw the tears in my eyes. She leaned in close.

I think she knew what my heart so desperately needed to know. I asked her, "Does this mean God can possibly forgive me for what I have done?" Is it possible for me to be free from my dark? Is it possible? All I wanted was a possibility. That day was my first glance within the open door of my heart that Jesus had been knocking on.

I am dark but lovely. What a thought that we can be both. We are both.

Jesus invites us into a relationship with Him. This invitation of dining with Him speaks of intimacy. He calls us, the very One who spoke and the heavens were created. He breathed the word and the stars were born. Psalm 33:6-7.

The One who sees my dark and calls me lovely.

It's time to open the door.

The Fairest of all is waiting on the other side.

In Revelation 4, John is shown an open door in heaven. This is just 2 verses after Jesus is telling us "Look! I stand at the door and knock."

In Revelation 6, John is invited 4 times to "Come and See."

I think the answer to the discovery of the One who is truly the Fairest of All is found behind the open door.

Ask Jesus any question you have.

"Do you truly delight in me?" Come and See!

"Do you have a purpose for my life?" Come and See!

"Am I beautiful in your sight?" Come and See!

"Do you hear me when I call?" Come and See!

"Will you carry my burdens?" Come and See!

"I cannot see the way out of this situation, can you?" Come and See!

"I am so lonely. Will you be with me?" Come and See!

"I have been hurt so badly. Can you heal me?" Come and See!

"Can you forgive me?" Come and See!

"Do you love me?" Come and See!

"Am I lovely?" Come and See!

Esther, who stood out in the midst of hundreds of beautiful women who were brought to the palace. The one in charge set her apart from the others. There was something different about her. It had nothing to do with her outward appearance, after all each of them had been chosen because of their stunning looks.

We often only focus on the outward appearance of people. We celebrate how they look.

Yet, God works not from the outside in but from the inside out.

Jesus came so we could have life and have it to the full. "If anyone is in Me, he is new creation, the old is gone and the new has come." I cling to this! That my "dark" can be gone!

I believe He starts with our heart. On our own, the heart is deceitful above all else. "The heart wants what the heart wants!" That will get you to regret faster than you can say, "Maybe I shouldn't have done that." This inside out transformation journey begins when we surrender our heart to the One who created it. It is then,

CHAPTER TEN - *THE FAIREST*

through the open door, I am invited to "Come and See" that He is enough, He is truth, Life, Redeemer, Refuge, Strength, Savior, Lord, and the lover of my soul.

I no longer need to chase a mirage. Jesus is right there waiting for me. He has always been right there, through every, "sand drinking" experience I have been through. I don't know what you have personally went through. Many of us have been through horrific things at the hands of others. I cannot answer your why. The only answer I have for brokenness, hurt, shame, and pain is Jesus.

Jesus -

The One who gave all so we could be given all He is.

The One whose love for you held Him to the cross. Nails were not necessary.

The One without blame, took the blame, so you could be free.

The One who experienced unimaginable pain so you would know He can carry yours.

The One who came for you, the thief on the cross, and offers paradise.

The One who would have done all of it for you alone. For you.

The One who is standing at the door of your heart asking to come in.

On our own, we will never be enough.

With the One, who is the Fairest of All, we are never on our own.

Peace Treaty

A peace treaty is an agreement between two or more hostile parties which formally ends a state of war, or conflict, between the parties.

An agreement to come to peace and end conflict.

An agreement to stop fighting.

To just stop fighting.

I was so tired of fighting.

I think we have all seen a treaty signing. It's a big deal. Both sides have been brought to the table because of the one, the go between, who has brokered this peace deal. Both sides seem genuinely happy to be there. They shake hands and smile as if they are new best friends. Surrounded by media, they each pick up their pen and sign their copy of the treaty. Those who have been involved in the fighting let out a deep sigh of relief. Finally, there can be peace.

Peace - this seemingly elusive, intangible feeling that escapes us.

Early last year, in the midst of the famous "mirror and scale" war, I had an epiphany. Here I was staring 56 in the face and realizing that I am closer to 60 than not. I didn't want to live the rest of my life in this battle. I was beat up, worn out, and oh so tired of losing the battles. I wanted off the rollercoaster, out of the wilderness, and the white flag thrown into the ring.

This epiphany was just a simple question. "What if I stopped living as if my body was the enemy?" Simple question but a huge one. What would my life look like if I lived this way? What would need to change to make this a reality? This one question required me to dig deep into my food challenges, body hatred, and self-pity party mindset I was in. I made a bold, albeit wrong, declaration. I decided to that I would daily say "I am at peace with my body."

For days I did this. I love daily affirmations. I use ones based on scripture daily. What a wonderful reminder of His truth! Yet, this whole name it and claim it of "I am at peace with my body" sounded great but nothing was happening. Why? What is wrong with me? "Why can't I?," and "How come I am not?" Truthfully, it wasn't very peaceful.

What is peace? Jesus tells us that His peace He gives us. His peace. I want that. In James, we are told to pursue peace with all people. That one hit me. I would like to tell you I do this, yet I pursue peace with others and would not treat them how I treat myself. How do I pursue peace with myself? The pursuit of peace needed to begin with an excavation project. I needed to dig deep into my why I eat the way I do. My triggers, the emotions involved, my past experiences, hurts, and losses. I needed to really look at how I got to this place. I truly needed to see the cost of change. All change costs something. We are told we must first count the cost before we build. This new way of thinking will cost me my old way of thinking. I wanted to cheer! The old is gone, but we tend to gravitate back to what we know, even if it is making us miserable.

CHAPTER ELEVEN - *PEACE TREATY*

I was tired of going back. I needed to ask myself "Do I want to be made well?" In Acts 3, where Peter and John come across this man who is seeking money, they offered him something else. They offered the opportunity to walk, to be made well, something he had not achieved before. Do I want what Jesus is offering me? His peace? His plan of action? Where the Spirit of the Lord is there is freedom. I wanted and desperately needed the freedom peace offered.

Remember, a peace treaty ends a conflict between two hostile parties. Yes, hostile parties. I was in a major, ongoing battle with myself and felt as if I was trapped behind enemy lines.

I needed to learn how to live at peace with me. I needed a peace treaty!

A Peace Treaty that defines the boundaries necessary for my wellbeing.

What lines do I need to draw with my eating choices, mindset, self-talk, activities, and actions?

What do I need to move towards and what do I need to move away from?

I clearly needed to reframe how I talked to myself and how I talked about myself. This "I am so fat," "I am so stupid," and "I have no willpower," needed to go and go now. I realized just how much of the conflict was in my mind. I was in desperate need of clearly defined boundaries. We are told to take every thought captive and line it up with the truth of God's word. I had spent years allowing the condemning thoughts to rule and I was declaring a coup!

I looked at my eating habits and didn't like what I saw. I was the queen of doing great and then falling off the cliff. Then I would beat myself up (and binge some more) over my failure. I didn't have a clue of why I ate the way I did. I didn't understand my triggers so I was an easy take down. In setting up boundaries in my eating choices, I needed to assess where the lines needed to be drawn. What was allowed in and what needed to be defended against. I was like a city with broken down walls. Unprotected and overrun.

It was time to ask the hard questions to define and build my boundaries.

Why do I eat the way I do?

How am I feeling when I am eating?

What food choices cause me to binge?

What situations are the hardest for me to stay within my boundaries?

What emotions trigger food responses?

Am I hiding my battle from others?

How will I react when I fall?

What needs to change in my mindset?

This didn't happen overnight. Yes, I stood up and declared I was at peace with myself but then the hard work began. I had to dig up, pull out, and dust off the deep-seated issues that were triggers I never realized. Only when exposed to the light could they begin to be dismantled. Yes, dismantling must happen so the rebuilding can begin!

Your boundaries must be protected. NO! must become a word you use. Wield well. I use it in the grocery store against different foods that want to jump in my cart and come home with me. I will not have a conversation with them any longer. The longer I stand there and look at them, the more likely they will jump in the cart and I will eat all of it on the way home. NO! Just say no and for goodness sake, walk away! I am choosing not to participate. I needed to reframe my words from "I can't eat that" (depravation) to "I am choosing not to" (power). I really thought others just had the market on willpower and I was absent the day they handed it out. Reality is that willpower is just a muscle. The more you use it, the stronger it gets. Willpower also is at its weakest when you are tired, emotional, and busy. We make our poorest decisions when we are spent. Guard it well and take good care of it.

Daily, choose to be at peace with you. Small, daily, seemingly insignificant improvements, and choices, when done with consistency (your new best friend!), over time produces amazing results! This peace treaty is not a "21 days to a new habit" gig, it's a daily walk in the discovery of living the rest of your life in the peace that passes all understanding and allowing that peace to guard your heart and mind. Choose today to pursue peace with yourself and to extend copious amounts of grace to yourself on the journey. Wrap yourself in the peace of God, which passes all understanding, allowing His peace to guard your hearts and minds.

Write. Your. Peace Treaty.

You are not your enemy. Your body isn't your enemy. Come out from behind the enemy lines. Ask yourself the hard questions. Take the time to explore the questions. Write the answers that come to mind. The template is merely a guide for you to use. Your peace treaty should be as individual as you are. Begin to dismantle the old and start defining your boundary lines. It does depend on you to pursue peace with you. The prison door is flung wide open and is waiting for you to walk through.

www.ingramcontent.com/pod-product-compliance
Lightning Source LLC
Chambersburg PA
CBHW052115110526
44592CB00013B/1622